GREAT MAP GAMES

20 Super Fun, Easy Reproducible Games That Build Key Map and Geography Skills— and Help Kids Navigate Their World!

by Susan Julio

SCHOLASTIC
PROFESSIONAL BOOKS

NEW YORK • TORONTO • LONDON • AUCKLAND • SYDNEY
MEXICO CITY • NEW DELHI • HONG KONG

To Peanut Shell
and Gummi-Bear

Cover design by James Sarfati
Interior design by Solutions by Design, Inc.
Maps by Jim McMahon
Illustrations by Dave Clegg

ISBN # 0-439-07753-2
Copyright © 2000 by Susan Julio

CONTENTS

ABOUT THIS BOOK

The 20 games in this book make learning about maps fun and challenging. As a learning tool, games help reinforce map-skill strategies while providing an atmosphere of enjoyment, stimulation, and cooperation in the classroom. The skills chosen for each game are based on the five standard themes of geography:

1. Location—the position of places and people

2. Place—physical and human characteristics of a specific region

3. Human—environment interactions; use and misuse of the environment

4. Movement—environmental changes

5. Region—unifying characteristics

HOW TO USE THIS BOOK

You'll find games that build basic map skills (such as location, direction, and distance) at the front of the book, and games that feature actual maps (road, street, landmark) at the back. Each game supplements and reinforces specific map-reading strategies that you may currently be teaching or have already taught in the classroom.

To introduce a new game to your class, show students the game and describe how it's played. Spark interest by inviting some students to play the game with you. Encourage students to play these map games independently during free time or whenever they have a few minutes to spare.

The games may be played by either two players, two or more players (in a small group setting), or the entire class (large group). For individual students who may be struggling with a specific mapping concept, consider sending a game home as a family-involved homework assignment.

You may also want to create a list of selected games that students can complete for extra credit. To celebrate the culmination of a map-unit study, set up game stations at various tables. Then, divide the students into groups and have them take turns visiting each station.

PREPARING TO PLAY

Inside this book, you'll find reproducible game boards, cards, and playing pieces necessary to play the different games. Each game also includes:

⊚ An overview of the map skill students will learn

⊚ Recommended number of players

⊚ Materials list

⊚ Simple student and teacher directions

⊚ An extension or variation to the game

Before handing out the games to students, you may want to prepare some of the game pieces:

Stand-alone Markers (for use in Strange Sightings, Special Delivery, Pony Express, Treasure Hunt, Scavenger Hunt, Around the World, Birds of a Feather, and Road Trip)

1. For each of the above games, photocopy the page that illustrates the markers (pages 16, 20, 28, 31, 41, 45, 60, 79).

2. Cut out the markers and their bases. Glue the figures and bases to oak tag for durability.

3. Cut along the dotted lines at the bottom of each marker and at the top of each base.

Slide the markers into their bases as shown.

Goliath Beetle
(Africa)

Number/Letter Cubes (for use in Special Delivery, Treasure Hunt, Ant Attack, Scavenger Hunt, Art Heist, and Road Trip)

1. For each of the above games, photocopy the page that illustrates the number and/or letter cube (pages 20, 31, 34, 41, 68, 79).

2. Cut out the cube along the dotted lines. Then fold along the solid lines and glue where indicated.

Spinners (for use in Strange Sightings and Treasure Hunt)

1. For each of the above games, photocopy the page that illustrates the spinner (pages 16 and 31). Cut out the spinner and glue it to oak tag.

2. Use a sharp pencil to punch a hole through the spinner's center. Place one end of a large paper clip over the hole. Then insert a brass fastener through the paper clip and hole. Bend the ends flat on the other side of the spinner. Make sure the paper clip can spin freely. Adjust the fastener as needed.

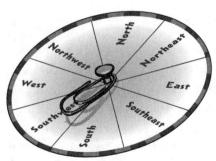

Game Cards (for use in Land-and-Water Bingo and Abbreviation Station)

1. For the Land-and-Water Bingo game, make at least five copies of the Bingo Card (page 10) and five copies of the Word Set (page 12). Cut apart one Word Set for each Bingo Card. Glue the words randomly on each space of the Bingo Card. Make sure the words are arranged differently on each card.

2. For the Abbreviation Station game, make four copies of the Abbreviation Station Game Card (page 22) and one copy of the Word Set (page 23). Cut apart the words and glue a word on each space of the game cards. Each card should have a different set of words.

WHO GOES FIRST?

Before each game, players will have to decide who takes the first turn. Players can either flip a coin (this works best for two players) or roll a number cube (for more than two players) to see who goes first. Game play should always go clockwise, or to the first player's left.

STORAGE TIPS

- Glue the game board to the inside of a file folder. Glue the directions to the other side. Use an envelope or small bag to hold game pieces.

- Place all game pieces (including directions) in a large manila envelope or sealable plastic bag. Label the envelope or bag with the name of the game, the skill it reinforces, the number of players suggested, and a contents list.

- Reproduce a number of games, complete with directions and game pieces. Store them in an accordion-type file, with each game labeled appropriately.

BIRD'S-EYE VIEW CONCENTRATION

When creating a map, mapmakers often draw objects as seen from a bird's point of view. Can you match the top view of different objects with their frontal view?

SKILL

Identify how objects might appear on a map

PLAYERS

2 or more

MATERIALS

⚙ Bird's-Eye View Concentration Cards

HOW TO PLAY

1. Shuffle the Bird's-Eye View Concentration Cards and place them facedown in five rows on a table.

2. Take turns uncovering two cards at a time. If you turn over two cards that show the front and top view of the same object, keep the cards and take another turn. If the cards don't match, turn the cards facedown again. The next player takes a turn.

3. Play continues until all matches have been made and no more cards remain. The player with the most matching pairs wins.

EXTENSION

Draw a detailed map of your neighborhood showing various structures and landmarks, such as houses and trees, as seen from above. How would your map be different if you drew the same objects as seen from the ground?

Great Map Games Scholastic Professional Books

BIRD'S-EYE VIEW

FRONT VIEW

BIRD'S-EYE VIEW

TOP VIEW

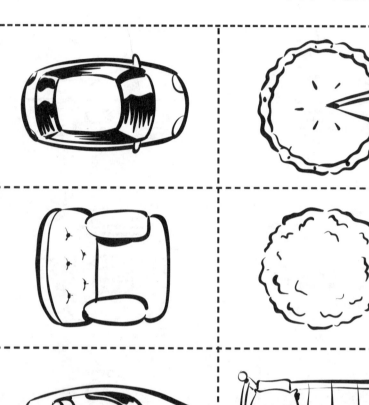

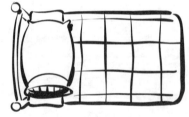

LAND-AND-WATER BINGO

What's the difference between a mountain and a hill, or a bay and a gulf? Find out when you play this bingo game that identifies Earth's various land and water formations.

SKILL

Identify land and water formations

PLAYERS

3 or more, plus a Caller

MATERIALS

- Land-and-Water Bingo Card* for each player
- 24 Space Markers (pennies or buttons) for each player
- Land-and-Water Definition Cards (cut apart and put in a bag)
- Answer Chart

HOW TO PLAY

1. The Caller distributes a bingo card and 24 space markers to each player. Players cover the FREE space on their card with one marker. The Caller holds on to the bag of Definition Cards and the Answer Chart.

2. The Caller draws a Definition Card from the bag, reads aloud the definition written on it, and shows the card to all players. Find the word on your bingo card that matches the definition. If you find it, cover the word with a marker. The Caller then places the card on the matching space on the Answer Chart.

3. The first player to get five markers in a row (vertically, diagonally, or horizontally) yells "Bingo!" The Caller uses the Answer Chart to check the player's covered words against those that were called. The player who matches the words and definitions correctly wins.

* See page 5 for instructions on how to prepare the Bingo Cards.

EXTENSION

Use the picture cards to make an illustrated map of your state's land and water formations.

LAND-AND-WATER

		FREE		

Great Map Games Scholastic Professional Books

LAND-AND-WATER

A narrow piece
of land that joins
two larger
pieces of land

A body of land
completely
surrounded
by water

An area of
mostly flat,
treeless land

A body of water
that connects
two bigger bodies
of water

A body of water
partly closed in
by land

The largest bodies
of salt water

A cone-shaped
opening on the
earth's surface that
spews ash, lava,
and gas

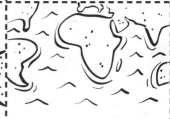

The largest of all
landforms

A large group of
islands clustered
together

A hill or mountain
with steep sides
and a flat top

A narrow flow of
water that connects
two bigger bodies
of water

A large area
of an ocean or a
sea partly closed in
by land. It is usually
bigger than a bay.

A raised,
rounded landform
that is lower than
a mountain

A large body of salt
water that is smaller
than an ocean

A landform
that rises high above
other land areas

A pointed piece of
land that stretches
out into the water.
It is smaller than
a peninsula.

LAND-AND-WATER

Land surrounded
by water on
three sides

A large stream of
water that empties
into another
body of water

A large body
of water that is
completely
surrounded by land

A river or stream
that joins
a larger one

A steep fall or flow
of water from a
high place

Low areas that
separate mountains
and hills

Muddy,
flat lowlands

A huge mass of ice
that moves slowly
down a slope or
spreads outward over
a land surface

WORD SET

Archipelago	Gulf	Mesa	Sea
Bay	Hill	Mountain	Strait
Cape	Island	Oceans	Tributary
Channel	Isthmus	Peninsula	Valleys
Continent	Lake	Plain	Volcano
Glacier	Marsh	River	Waterfall

Great Map Games Scholastic Professional Books

LAND-AND-WATER

A narrow piece of land that joins two larger pieces of land (Isthmus)	A body of land completely surrounded by water (Island)	An area of mostly flat, treeless land (Plain)	A body of water that connects two bigger bodies of water (Channel)
A body of water partly closed in by land (Bay)	The largest bodies of salt water (Oceans)	A cone-shaped opening on the earth's surface that spews ash, lava, and gas (Volcano)	The largest of all landforms (Continent)
A large group of islands clustered together (Archipelago)	A hill or mountain with steep sides and a flat top (Mesa)	A narrow flow of water that connects two bigger bodies of water (Strait)	A large area of an ocean or a sea partly closed in by land. It is usually bigger than a bay. (Gulf)
A raised, rounded landform that is lower than a mountain (Hill)	A large body of salt water that is smaller than an ocean (Sea)	A landform that rises high above other land areas (Mountain)	A pointed piece of land that stretches out into the water. It is smaller than a peninsula. (Cape)
Land surrounded by water on three sides (Peninsula)	A large stream of water that empties into another body of water (River)	A large body of water that is completely surrounded by land (Lake)	A river or stream that joins a larger one (Tributary)
A steep fall or flow of water from a high place (Waterfall)	Low areas that separate mountains and hills (Valleys)	Muddy, flat lowlands (Marsh)	A huge mass of ice that moves slowly down a slope or spreads outward over a land surface (Glacier)

Great Map Games Scholastic Professional Books

STRANGE SIGHTINGS

Strange and exotic creatures lurk in the continents of Asia, Africa, North America, South America, Antarctica, Europe, and Australia. Some have been sighted swimming in the Pacific, Atlantic, Indian, and Arctic oceans. How many of these creatures can you collect?

SKILL

Identify and locate the seven continents and four oceans

PLAYERS

2

MATERIALS

- Strange Sightings Game Board
- Creature Figures
- True-or-False Cards
- Spinner

HOW TO PLAY

1. Place each Creature Figure in the appropriate continent or ocean. Stack the True-or-False cards facedown within easy reach of both players.

2. Take turns spinning the spinner and following the directions on the spinner. If the spinner lands on "True or False," the other player draws a card from the stack and reads the statement written on it. Decide whether the statement is true or false. (Answers are at the bottom of the card.) If you answer correctly, take a Creature from the game board. If not, the other player reads aloud the correct answer and returns the card to the bottom of the pile. The other player takes a turn.

3. Play continues until all the Creatures have been taken from the board. The player with the most Creatures wins.

EXTENSION

Do research about the animals featured in this game. Find interesting facts about each animal and write them on separate True-or-False cards. Use them the next time you play the game.

Great Map Games Scholastic Professional Books

STRANGE SIGHTINGS

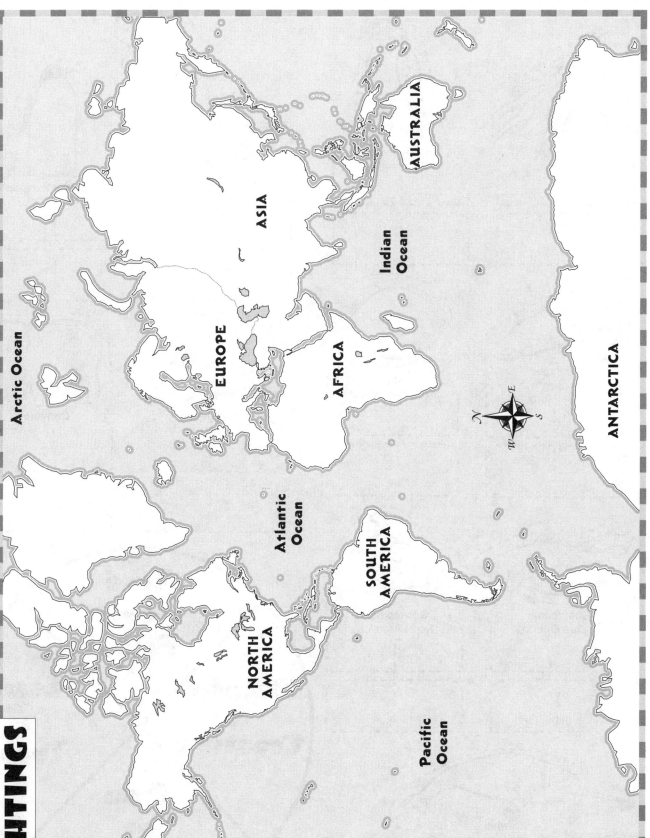

ARCTIC OCEAN

ASIA

AUSTRALIA

EUROPE

Indian Ocean

AFRICA

ANTARCTICA

Atlantic Ocean

NORTH AMERICA

SOUTH AMERICA

Pacific Ocean

Great Map Games Scholastic Professional Books

STRANGE SIGHTINGS

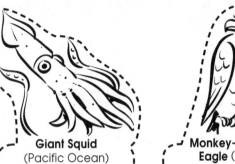

Giant Squid
(Pacific Ocean)

**Monkey-eating
Eagle** (Asia)

Assemble markers
as shown.

Goliath Beetle
(Africa)

Emperor Penguin
(Antarctica)

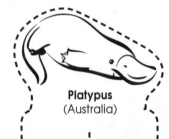

Platypus
(Australia)

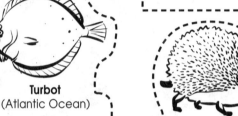

Turbot
(Atlantic Ocean)

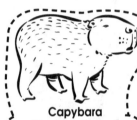

Hedgehog
(Europe)

Capybara
(South America)

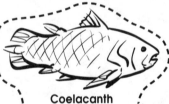

Coelacanth
(Indian Ocean)

Gila Monster
(North America)

**True
or
False**

**Return
a
Creature**

**Lose
a
Turn**

**True
or
False**

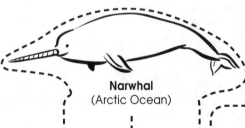

Narwhal
(Arctic Ocean)

Great Map Games
Scholastic Professional Books

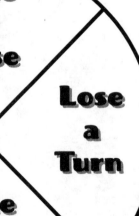

STRANGE SIGHTINGS

Continents are the largest landforms. (True)	There are four major continents. (False. There are seven continents.)	The largest continent is Antarctica. (False. Asia is the largest continent.)
Antarctica is a desert. (True)	Australia is the only country that is also a continent. (True)	Europe is the smallest continent. (False. Australia is the smallest continent.)
North America is the third-largest continent. (True)	Mexico and the United States are part of South America. (False. Mexico and the U.S. are part of North America.)	South America is the second-largest continent. (False. South America is the fourth-largest continent; Africa is the second.)
Europe is a continent between the Atlantic Ocean and Asia. (True)	Africa has the world's largest desert. (True)	Oceans are the largest bodies of water. (True)
There are seven oceans. (False. There are four oceans.)	Oceans are made of salt water. (True)	The largest ocean is the Pacific Ocean. (True)
Water covers half of the Earth's surface. (False. Water covers 3/4 of the Earth's surface.)	The Arctic is the shallowest and smallest ocean. (True)	The Pacific and Indian oceans surround Africa. (False. The Atlantic and Indian oceans surround Africa.)

Great Map Games *Scholastic Professional Books*

SPECIAL DELIVERY!

Some letters at the Post Office have postal workers stumped! The letters don't have addresses written on them. Instead, they're stamped with *map symbols* (small pictures or signs that stand for a place) that show where each letter goes. Can you guess what the symbols mean and deliver each letter to the correct address?

S K I L L

Interpreting map symbols

P L A Y E R S

Up to 4

M A T E R I A L S

- ✪ Special Delivery Game Board
- ✪ Number Cube
- ✪ Letters
- ✪ Mail Truck Marker for each player

POST OFFICE

E X T E N S I O N

Create a scrapbook that shows the various symbols that you've seen, such as street or road signs. Draw each symbol on your scrapbook and write what the symbol stands for next to it. How many symbols can you find?

H O W   T O   P L A Y

1. Shuffle the Letters and distribute them evenly among the players. Each player chooses a numbered Mail Truck and places it on the corresponding number space on the game board.

2. Take turns rolling the number cube to move your Mail Truck clockwise around the game board. If you land on a place space (for example, ferry), decide if one of your Letters bears the symbol for that place. For instance, say the symbol F stands for ferry. If you have a Letter stamped with the correct symbol, "deliver," or leave, the Letter in that space. If you land in a Red Letter! space, move to any symbol space you choose. (You may want to move to a space where you can leave a Letter.) The next player takes a turn.

3. Players continue around the game board until they have delivered all their Letters. When you've delivered all your Letters, roll the number cube to get back to your number space and, from there, to the Post Office. The player who delivers all of his or her Letters and reaches the Post Office first wins.

SPECIAL DELIVERY!

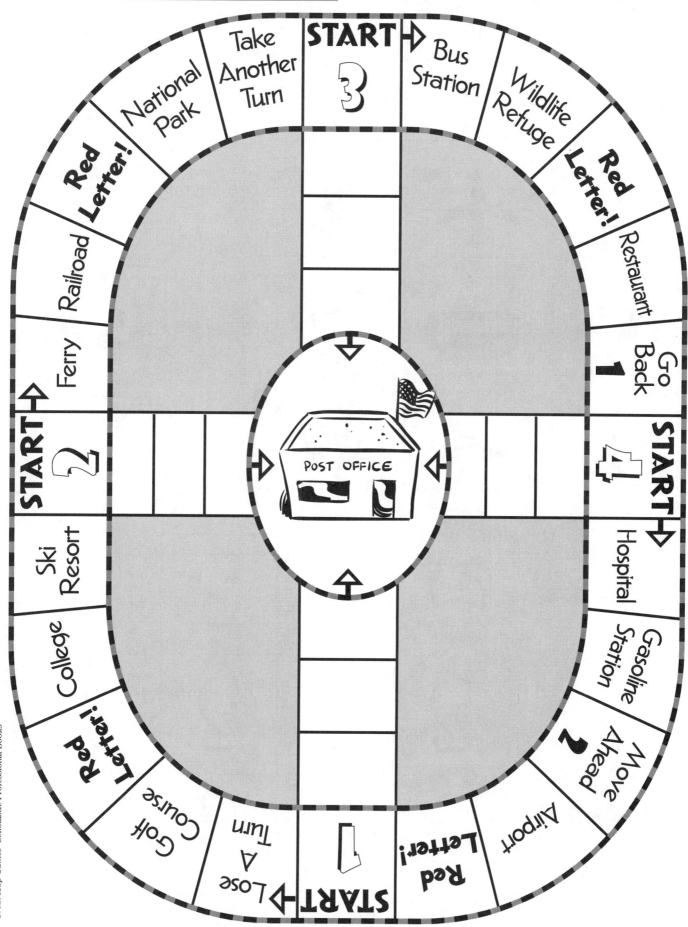

START 3

Bus Station

Wildlife Refuge

Red Letter!

Restaurant

Go Back 1

START 4

Hospital

Gasoline Station

Move Ahead 2

Airport

Red Letter!

START 1

Lose A Turn

Golf Course

Red Letter!

College

Ski Resort

START 2

Ferry

Railroad

Red Letter!

National Park

Take Another Turn

POST OFFICE

SPECIAL DELIVERY!

MAIL
1

MAIL
2

MAIL
3

Assemble markers
as shown.

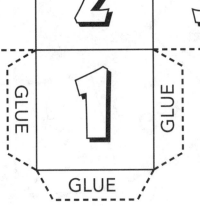

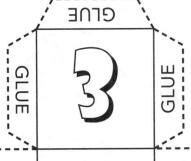

MAIL
4

Great Map Games Scholastic Professional Books

ABBREVIATION STATION

All aboard the Shortcut Express! Did you know that mapmakers often *abbreviate*, or shorten, words on maps to save space? Get on the right track by filling your "train yard" with the correct abbreviation "trains."

SKILL

Identify map abbreviations

PLAYERS

Up to 4 players

MATERIALS

- Abbreviation Station Game Card* for each player
- Abbreviation Train Cards

HOW TO PLAY

1. Put the Abbreviation Train cards in a bag or envelope. Each Abbreviation Train card features an abbreviation that matches a word on one of the Abbreviation Station game cards.

2. Each player selects an Abbreviation Station game card. Take turns drawing a Train card. If you pick a Train card that matches a word on your Station card, "park" the train over the word. (Players must agree that the abbreviation and word match.) If there's no match, put the Train card back in the bag. The next player takes a turn.

3. The first player to cover all the words on his or her game card wins.

* See page 5 for instructions on how to prepare the game cards.

EXTENSION

Look at a map of your state or county. Count how many abbreviations you see. What do they stand for?

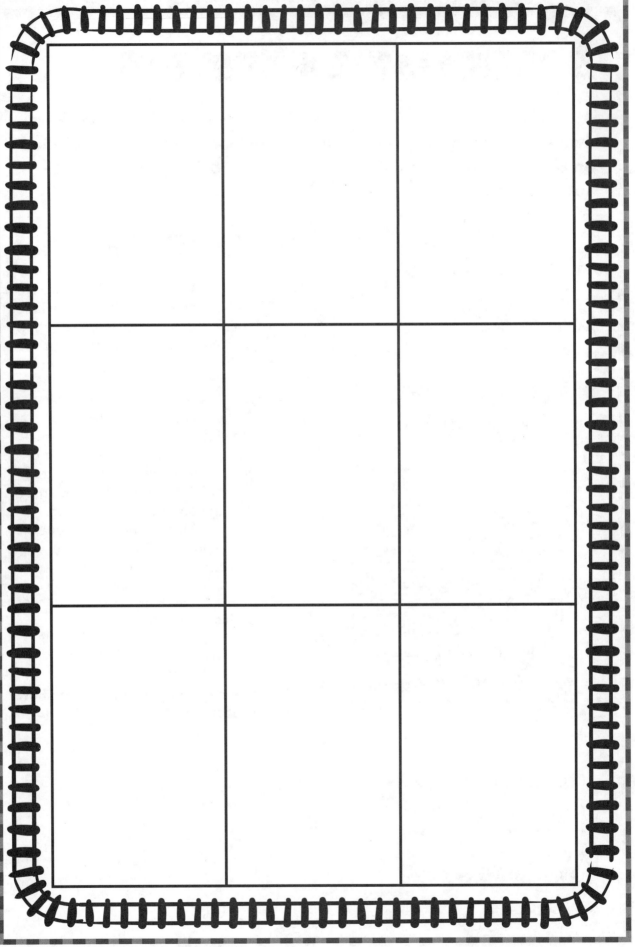

GAME CARD

ABBREVIATION STATION

Great Map Games Scholastic Professional Books

Avenue	**Boulevard**	**County**	**Drive**
East	**Fort**	**Highway**	**International**
Island	**Junction**	**Lane**	**Library**
Mountain	**National**	**North**	**Northeast**
Northwest	**Park**	**Parkway**	**Point**
Post Office	**Province**	**Railroad**	**Republic**
River	**Road**	**Route**	**School**
South	**Southeast**	**Southwest**	**Station**
Street	**Township**	**Turnpike**	**West**

Ave.	Blvd.	Co.	Dr.
E	Ft.	Hwy.	Intl.
Isl.	Jct.	Ln.	Lib.
Mt.	Natl.	N	NE
NW	Pk.	Pkwy.	Pt.
P.O.	Prov.	RR	Rep.
Riv.	Rd.	Rte.	Sch.
S	SE	SW	Sta.
St.	Twp.	Tpke.	W

Great Map Games Scholastic Professional Books

PONY EXPRESS

In 1860, the government created the *Pony Express*—a mail-delivery service that used fast horses and riders—to relay news and mail to the Western states. Mail carriers rode for about 10 days to get from Saint Joseph, Missouri, to Sacramento, California. How fast can you get to Sacramento?

SKILL

Use scale to measure distance

PLAYERS

Up to 3 players, plus a Postmaster

MATERIALS

- Pony Express Game Board
- Horse Marker for each player
- Mileage Marker for each player
- Route Card for each player
- Answer Key

Geographically Speaking...

The original Pony Express traveled from St. Joseph, Missouri, along the Little Blue River to Fort Kearney, Nebraska. From there, the route continued up the Platte River to Fort Laramie, Wyoming, then along the Sweetwater River to Fort Caspar, Wyoming. Riders then proceeded to Salt Lake City, Utah, across the desert and over the Sierra Nevada mountains, until they reached Sacramento, California. A steamer carried the mail across the Sacramento River to San Francisco. The entire Pony Express Trail was nearly 2,000 miles long.

HOW TO PLAY

1. Each player chooses a Route Card, Mileage marker, and Horse marker. Each Route Card lists an imaginary route that the player must follow. The Postmaster holds the Answer Key.

2. Place the Horses on St. Joseph, Missouri—the starting point of the Pony Express. Take turns estimating the distance between two cities and moving your Horse.

3. To play, estimate **to the nearest 100 miles** the distance between St. Joseph and the first stop on your Route Card. Then use the Mileage marker to measure the correct distance (see How to Measure Routes, next page). The Postmaster checks the Answer Key to see whether or not you're correct. If you estimate correctly (within 100 miles of the actual mileage), move your Horse to the first town. If not, stay in place and wait until your next turn to give the correct mileage and move your Horse. The next player takes a turn.

4. Play continues with each player taking turns estimating and moving his or her Horse along the routes. The first player to reach Sacramento, California, wins.

How to Measure Routes:

Most maps include a "Scale of Miles" to help readers estimate the distance between places. The scale shows the relationship between a distance on the map and the actual distance on the ground. Because a map is a small representation of a place, an inch on the map may represent 100 miles.

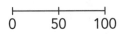

0   50   100

To measure the distance between two towns, lay your Mileage marker along the route you wish to measure. For

EXTENSION

Make new Route cards between St. Joseph, Missouri, and Sacramento, California. Find the shortest route between the two cities.

example, say you want to calculate the distance between Denver and Santa Fe. Place one end of your Mileage marker at Denver and point the other end toward Santa Fe. The distance between the two places is about 300 miles.

ROUTE #1

St. Joseph, MO, to
Dallas, TX

Dallas, TX, to
Santa Fe, NM

Santa Fe, NM, to
Phoenix, AZ

Phoenix, AZ, to
Los Angeles, CA

Los Angeles, CA, to
Sacramento, CA

ROUTE #2

St. Joseph, MO, to
Denver, CO

Denver, CO, to
Ft. Collins, CO

Ft. Collins, CO, to
Salt Lake City, UT

Salt Lake City, UT, to
Carson City, NV

Carson City, NV, to
Sacramento, CA

ROUTE #3

St. Joseph, MO, to
Ft. Kearney, NE

Ft. Kearney, NE, to
Great Falls, MT

Great Falls, MT, to
Seattle, WA

Seattle, WA, to
Placerville, CA

Placerville, CA, to
Sacramento, CA

Great Map Games Scholastic Professional Books

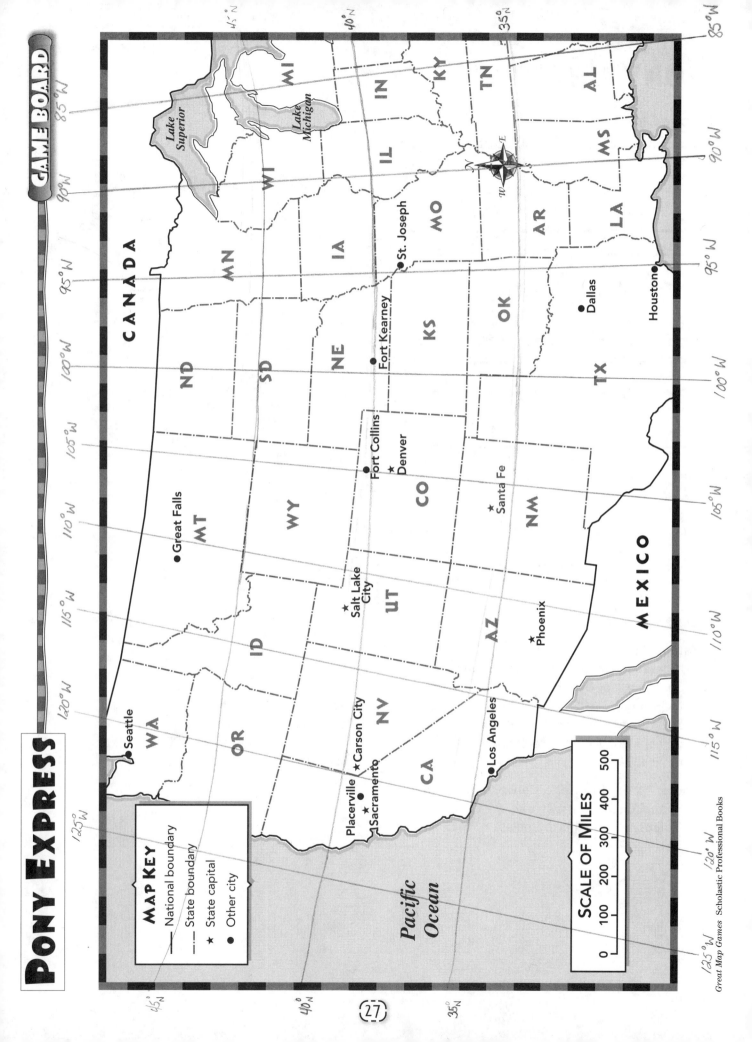

PONY EXPRESS

MAP KEY

— National boundary

--- State boundary

★ State capital

● Other city

SCALE OF MILES

0 100 200 300 400 500

CANADA

MEXICO

Pacific Ocean

Lake Superior

Lake Michigan

WA
OR
CA
NV
ID
MT
WY
UT
AZ
NM
CO
ND
SD
NE
KS
OK
TX
MN
IA
MO
AR
LA
WI
IL
MI
IN
KY
TN
MS
AL

● Seattle
● Great Falls
★ Carson City
★ Sacramento
Placerville
● Los Angeles
★ Phoenix
★ Salt Lake City
Fort Collins ●
Denver
★ Santa Fe
Fort Kearney ●
● St. Joseph
● Dallas
Houston ●

45° N
40° N
35° N

85° W
90° W
95° W
100° W
105° W
110° W
115° W
120° W
125° W

Great Map Games Scholastic Professional Books

PONY EXPRESS

Mileage Markers

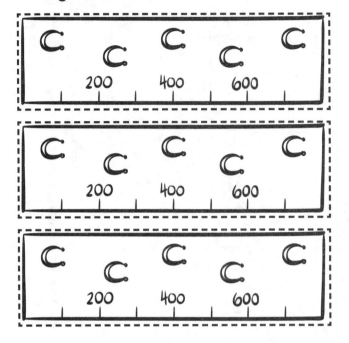

Assemble markers as shown.

Answer Key

(Distance calculated "as the crow flies.")

Route #1: St. Joseph to Dallas, ~500 miles (actual distance is 492 miles) • Dallas to Santa Fe, ~600 miles (562 miles) • Santa Fe to Phoenix, ~400 miles (378 miles) • Phoenix to Los Angeles, ~400 miles (367 miles) • Los Angeles to Sacramento, ~400 miles (351 miles)

Route #2: St. Joseph to Denver, ~500 miles (actual distance is 535 miles) • Denver to Ft. Collins, ~100 miles (55 miles) • Ft. Collins to

Salt Lake City, ~400 miles (361 miles) • Salt Lake City to Carson City, ~400 miles (430 miles) • Carson City to Sacramento, ~100 miles (101 miles)

Route #3: St. Joseph to Ft. Kearney, ~200 miles (actual distance is 235 miles) • Ft. Kearney to Great Falls, ~800 miles (766 miles) • Great Falls to Seattle, ~500 miles (517 miles) • Seattle to Placerville, ~600 miles (619 miles) • Placerville to Sacramento, ~0 miles (38 miles)

Great Map Games Scholastic Professional Books

TREASURE HUNT!

Do you go around in circles trying to figure out which way is north? A *compass rose* on a map can help. This circular or starlike symbol points the way to north, south, east, or west, and all other directions in between, such as northeast or southwest. Follow compass directions to find your treasure!

SKILL

Use cardinal and intercardinal directions to locate position

PLAYERS

2

MATERIALS

- ✿ Treasure Hunt Game Board
- ✿ Pirate Figure for each player
- ✿ 2 Treasure Chest Markers for each player
- ✿ Direction Spinner
- ✿ Number Cube

EXTENSION

Write directions to your house from school using compass directions. For example, when you walk out the school door, walk north for two blocks, then west for one block. Give a friend your written directions to see if he or she can follow it to your home.

HOW TO PLAY

1. Each player picks two Treasure Chests and writes his or her initials on them. Players then take each other's Treasure Chests and place them in any two squares on the game board.

2. Each player picks a Pirate and places it at the space marked "START."

3. Players take turns rolling the number cube to find out how many spaces to move. To find out in which direction to move, spin the Direction spinner. If you roll a 3 and spin north, for example, move 3 squares up. (North and south directions move up and down, east and west move right and left, and northeast, northwest, southeast, and southwest move diagonally.) The map's compass rose can help you figure out in which direction to go. *NOTE: You can move to a space only if it's empty. If a Pirate already occupies the space, you must wait for your next turn.* The other player takes a turn.

4. The first player to land on a square that contains one of his or her own Treasure Chests wins the game.

TREASURE HUNT!

Shipwreck Beach

Parrot Point

START

Doubloon Lagoon

Pirate Cove

Pirate Island

NW N NE
W   E
SW S SE

Great Map Games Scholastic Professional Books

TREASURE HUNT!

Assemble markers as shown.

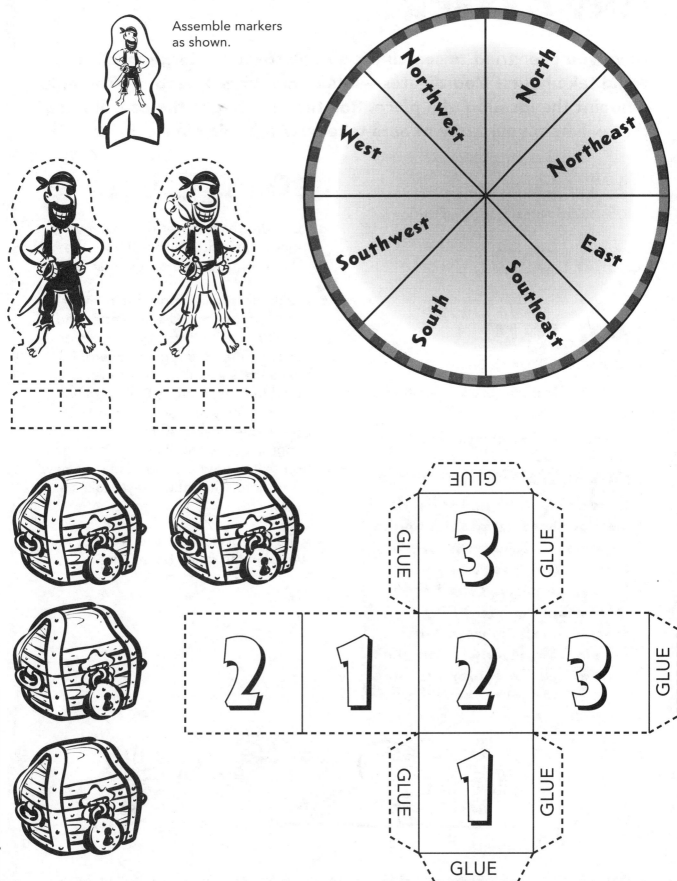

North
Northwest
Northeast
West
East
Southwest
Southeast
South

3
GLUE
GLUE
GLUE
2 1 2 3 GLUE
GLUE
1
GLUE
GLUE

ANT ATTACK!

Have you ever tried to search for a small town in a large map? It could take hours! *Coordinates*—sets of numbers or letters—can help pinpoint the location of a place. Roll the dice to get the coordinates that will help your army of ants take over a picnic blanket!

SKILL

Use coordinates to locate position

PLAYERS

2

MATERIALS

- ❀ Ant Attack Game Board
- ❀ 10 Ant Markers (black or white) for each player
- ❀ Number and Letter Cubes

VARIATION

Reverse the rules and place all Ants on coordinate spaces on the game board. Take turns rolling both cubes and *removing* Ants from those spaces. (The Ants' color doesn't matter.) Play continues until no more Ants remain. The player with the most Ants at the end of play wins.

HOW TO PLAY

1. Decide which player will have the Black Ants and which will have the White Ants. Divide up the markers.

2. Take turns rolling both the number and letter cubes. Use the letter and number to find the ordered pair, or *coordinate*, on the game board. For instance, say you roll a B and a 5. Find the second row, B, then move across until you reach column 5. Then place one of your Ants on the coordinate space. If an Ant is already on that coordinate, don't place a new Ant there. The other player takes a turn.

3. The first player to place all his or her Ants on the game board wins.

Great Map Games Scholastic Professional Books

ANT ATTACK!

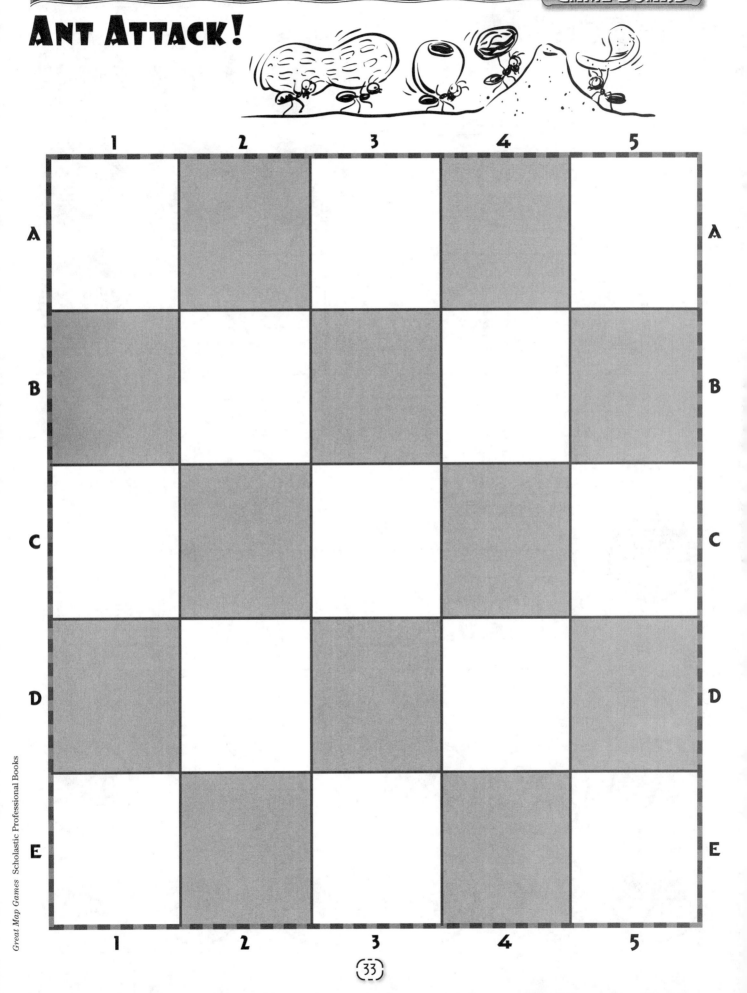

ANT ATTACK!

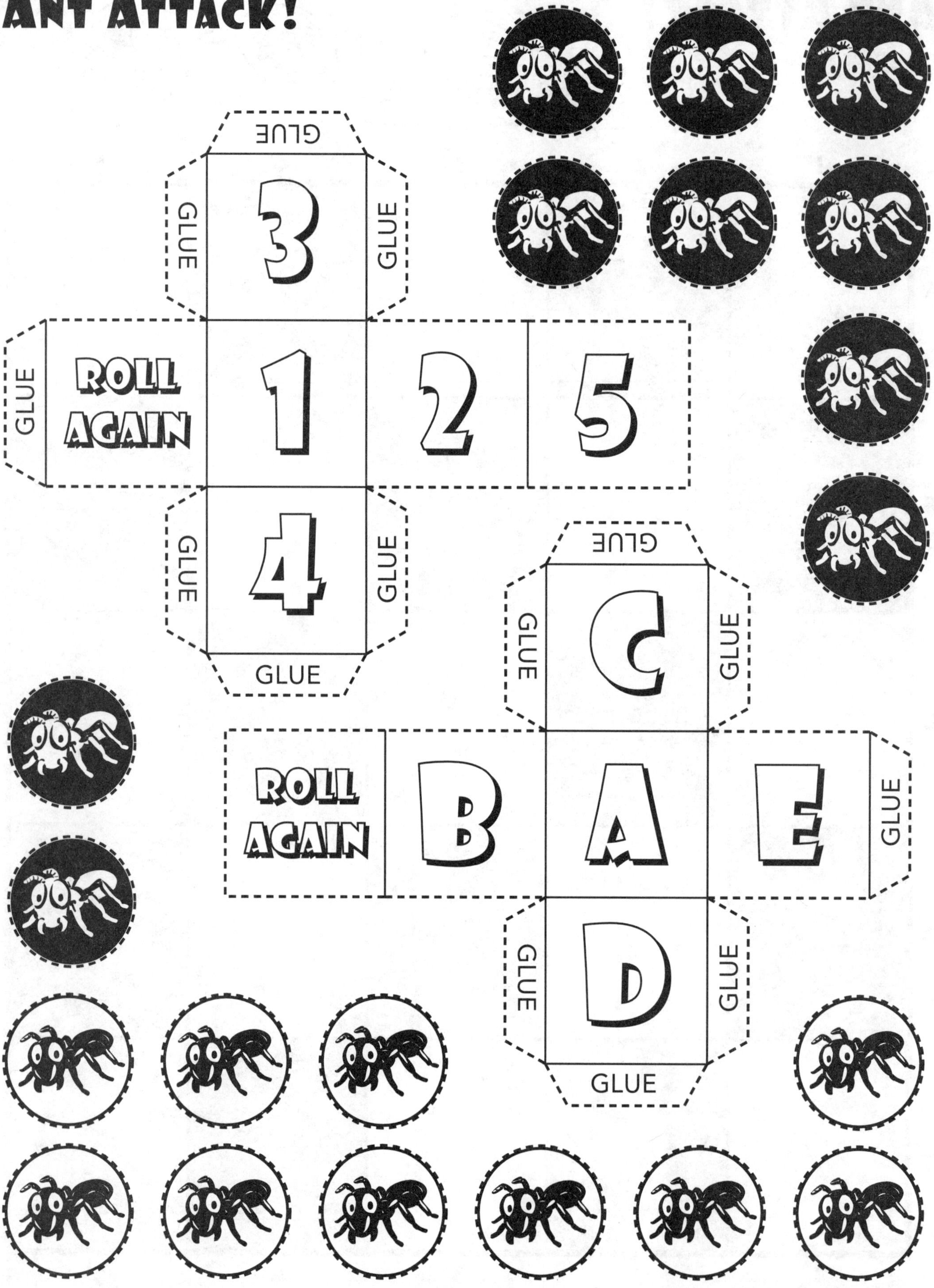

3

GLUE
GLUE
GLUE

ROLL AGAIN **1** **2** **5**

GLUE

GLUE **4** GLUE

GLUE

C

GLUE
GLUE
GLUE

ROLL AGAIN **B** **A** **E**

GLUE

GLUE **D** GLUE

GLUE

Great Map Games Scholastic Professional Books

MESSAGE IN A BOTTLE

Shipwrecked! Passengers of *Titanica* barely escaped the sinking ship. Luckily, they were able to swim to nearby deserted islands. Waiting to be rescued, survivors tossed bottles containing their *longitude* and *latitude* coordinates into the ocean. Use the coordinates to locate and rescue as many castaways as you can!

SKILL

Use longitude and latitude to locate position

PLAYERS

2

MATERIALS

- ✪ Message-in-a-Bottle Game Board
- ✪ Longitude and Latitude Cards (cut apart and put in separate envelopes labeled Longitude and Latitude)
- ✪ 20 Castaway Markers (pennies)

Geographically Speaking...

The equator (0°) is the starting point for measuring *latitude*. Latitude lines run parallel to the equator. Latitude lines above the equator are marked with an N for north, while latitude lines running below the equator are labeled with an S for south. The prime meridian (0°) is the starting point for measuring *longitude*. Longitude lines to the right of the prime meridian are marked E for east, and those on the left are marked W for west.

HOW TO PLAY

1. Place the Castaways on the deserted islands on the game board.

2. Players take turns drawing one Longitude and one Latitude card from each envelope. Using the coordinates, find where the longitude and latitude lines cross. For example, if you draw 25°E and 30°S cards, find where those two lines cross. If the lines meet over an island with a Castaway, "rescue," or take, the Castaway. Return the cards to their envelopes. The other player takes a turn.

3. Play continues until all Castaways have been rescued. The player who collects the most Castaways wins.

EXTENSION

Find the longitude and latitude coordinates of the different state capitals. Then challenge friends to guess which state capital belongs with each coordinate.

Message In a Bottle

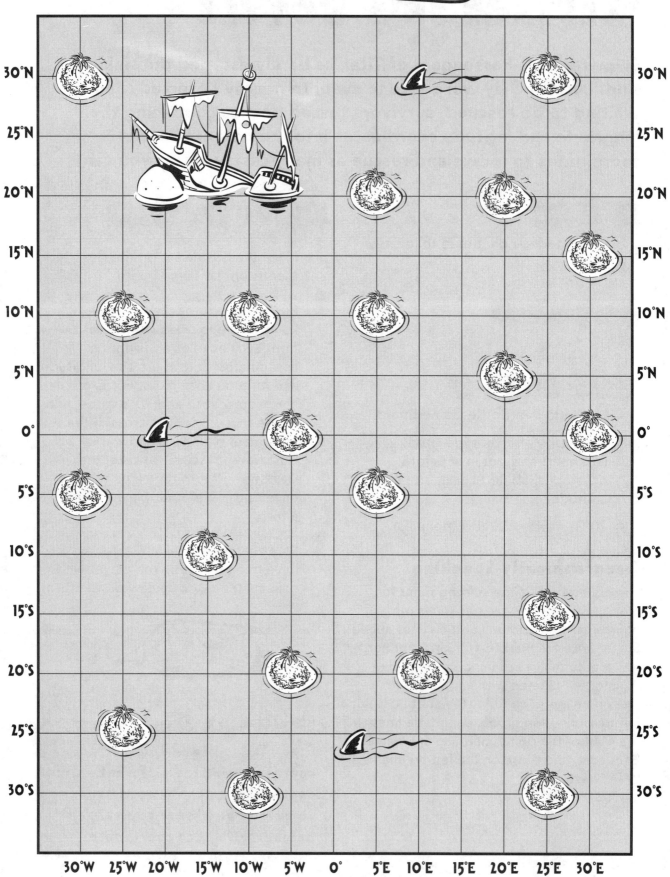

MESSAGE IN A BOTTLE

Longitude Cards

30°E	**25°E**	**20°E**

15°E	**10°E**	**5°E**	**0°**
5°W	**10°W**	**15°W**	**20°W**

25°W	**30°W**

30°N

Latitude Cards

25°N	**20°N**	**15°N**	**10°N**
5°N	**0°**	**5°S**	**10°S**
15°S	**20°S**	**25°S**	**30°S**

SCAVENGER HUNT

Aliens from outer space have come to Earth to study our *natural resources*—things provided by nature, like water or trees, that are useful to us. Now the aliens are on a scavenger hunt to track down the resources used to make some manufactured items. Can you help them find what they need?

SKILL

Read a key to identify natural resources

PLAYERS

Up to 4, plus a Space Inspector

MATERIALS

- Scavenger Hunt Game Board
- Alien Marker for each player
- Resource Card for each player
- Number Cube
- Answer Key

HOW TO PLAY

1. Each player chooses a numbered Alien and a Resource Card. The Space Inspector holds the Answer Key. Players place their Alien on the corresponding numbered Mother Ship (starting point).

2. Each Resource Card features six items that were made using natural resources. The Aliens must "collect" at least one natural resource for each item on their cards. (Each item may have been made from more than one resource.) Use the key in the middle of the game board to identify the different natural-resources symbols.

3. Take turns rolling the number cube to find out how many spaces to move the Alien. (Move clockwise around the game board.) If you land on a space with a natural-resources symbol, decide if that resource was used to make one of the items on your Resource Card. The Space Inspector checks the Answer Key to see if you're correct. If you are, cross off the item from your card. The next player takes a turn.

4. Play continues until a player has marked off all the items on his or her card, and gets back to the Mother Ship. The first player to return to his or her own Mother Ship with a completed Resource Card wins.

EXTENSION

Make new Resource Cards. Cut out photos from magazines of things made from the natural resources pictured on the game board. Then use the new cards next time you play the game.

Great Map Games *Scholastic Professional Books*

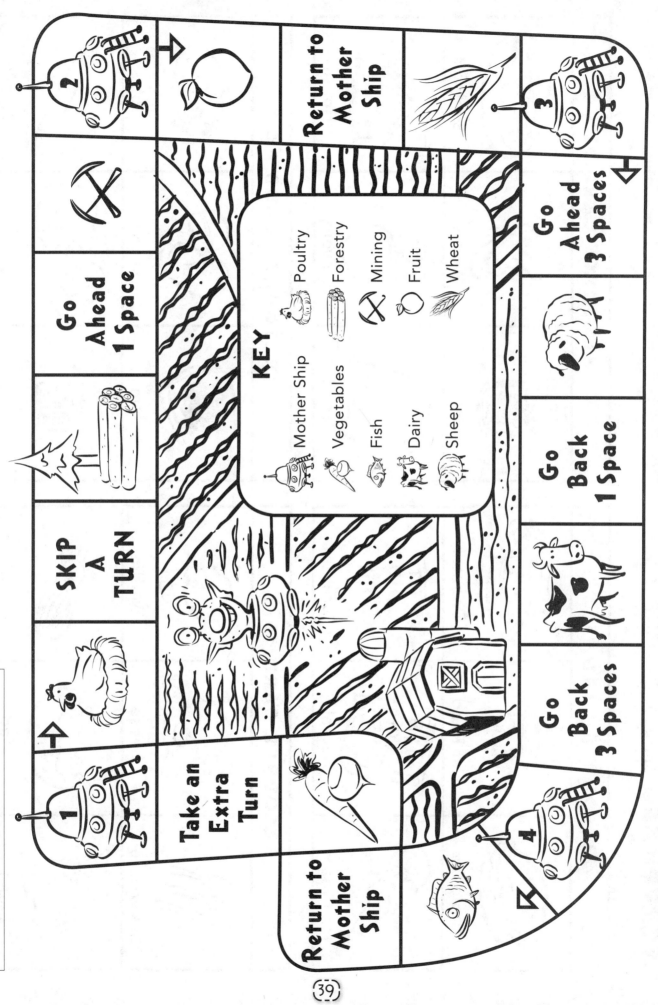

Scavenger Hunt

GAME BOARD

KEY

- Mother Ship
- Vegetables
- Fish
- Dairy
- Sheep
- Poultry
- Forestry
- Mining
- Fruit
- Wheat

Return to Mother Ship

Go Ahead 3 Spaces

Go Back 1 Space

Go Back 3 Spaces

Go Ahead 1 Space

SKIP A TURN

Take an Extra Turn

Return to Mother Ship

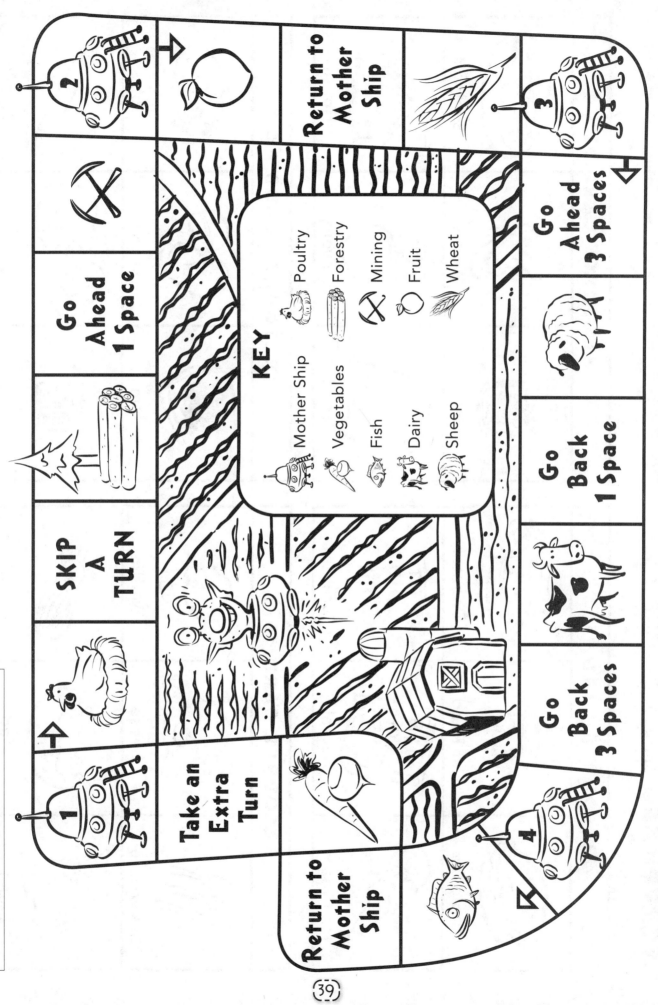

39

Great Map Games Scholastic Professional Books

RESOURCE CARDS

RESOURCE CARD #1

Apple Pie	Cat Food	Sweater
Ice Cream	Cereal	Furniture

RESOURCE CARD #2

Jelly	Socks	Seafood
Bread	Jewelry	House

RESOURCE CARD #3

Silverware	Cheese	Muffin
Paper	Salad	Yarn

RESOURCE CARD #4

Jam	Mittens	Coins
Soup	Eggs	Pencil

40

Great Map Games Scholastic Professional Books

SCAVENGER HUNT

Assemble markers as shown.

1 2 3

GLUE GLUE

GLUE 1 2 3 GLUE

GLUE GLUE

3

GLUE

Answer Key

RESOURCE CARD #1: Apple pie: fruit, wheat
• **Cat food:** poultry, fish, dairy, mining (can)
• **Sweater:** sheep • **Ice cream:** dairy, fruit •
Cereal: wheat, forestry (cereal box) •
Furniture: forestry

RESOURCE CARD #2: Jelly: fruit • **Socks:**
sheep • **Seafood:** fish • **Bread:** wheat •
Jewelry: mining • **House:** forestry (wood),
mining (metal frames)

RESOURCE CARD #3: Silverware: mining •
Cheese: dairy • **Muffin:** wheat, fruit, dairy •
Paper: forestry • **Salad:** vegetables, fruit •
Yarn: sheep

RESOURCE CARD #4: Jam: fruit • **Mittens:**
sheep • **Coins:** mining • **Soup:** vegetable,
fish, dairy, poultry, mining (can) • **Eggs:**
poultry • **Pencil:** forestry (wood), mining
(lead)

Great Map Games Scholastic Professional Books

AROUND THE WORLD

Various places around the world experience different kinds of weather—hot and sunny, cold and snowy, warm and muggy. To describe weather patterns that stay the same for a long period of time over a particular place, we use the word *climate*. Do you know what kind of climate you live in?

SKILL

Identify climate

PLAYERS

2

MATERIALS

- Around-the-World Game Board
- Jet Marker for each player
- Around-the-World Question Cards

Geographically Speaking . . .

The Earth is divided into three broad climate zones: tropical, temperate, and polar. The tropical region lies between the Tropic of Cancer and the Tropic of Capricorn, imaginary lines above and below the equator. The temperate regions are located between the Tropic of Cancer and the Arctic Circle, and between the Tropic of Capricorn and the Antarctic Circle. The polar regions cover the North Pole starting from the Arctic Circle, and the South Pole beginning at the Antarctic Circle.

EXTENSION

Pick a country in one of the three climates. Draw a picture showing the clothes, house, and food a person from that region would use.

HOW TO PLAY

1. Shuffle the Around-the-World Question Cards and stack them facedown in a pile. Park your Jets on START on the game board.

2. Take turns picking a Question Card and asking each other questions. If you answer correctly, move your Jet forward one space. (Move clockwise around the game board.) If not, the other player reads aloud the correct answer and returns the card to the bottom of the pile. The other player takes a turn.

3. The first player to go around the world and reach FINISH wins.

Great Map Games Scholastic Professional Books

AROUND THE WORLD

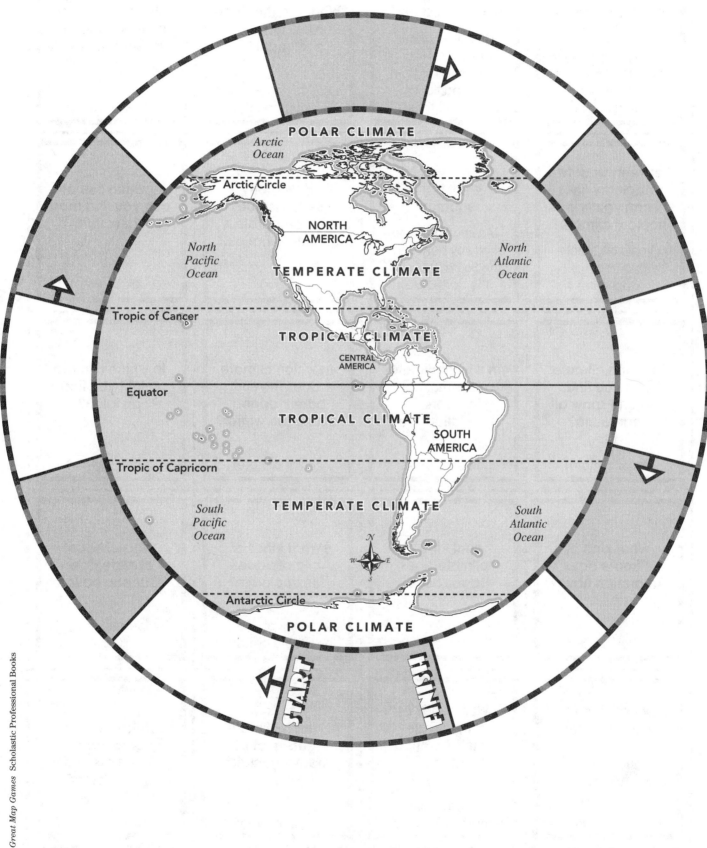

POLAR CLIMATE

Arctic
Ocean

Arctic Circle

NORTH
AMERICA

North
Pacific
Ocean

North
Atlantic
Ocean

TEMPERATE CLIMATE

Tropic of Cancer

TROPICAL CLIMATE

CENTRAL
AMERICA

Equator

TROPICAL CLIMATE

SOUTH
AMERICA

Tropic of Capricorn

TEMPERATE CLIMATE

South
Pacific
Ocean

South
Atlantic
Ocean

Antarctic Circle

POLAR CLIMATE

START

FINISH

What is climate?

(The typical weather pattern of a place over a long period of time)

What is weather?

(The state of the atmosphere—dry or rainy, hot or cold— at a particular place or time)

What are the three main types of climate?

(Polar, temperate, and tropical)

What imaginary line receives the most direct rays from the sun?

(The equator)

Between what two imaginary lines can you find tropical climate?

(Tropic of Cancer and Tropic of Capricorn)

What is the equator?

(An imaginary line halfway between the South Pole and the North Pole)

How many seasons does a temperate climate have?

(Four)

In which climate can you find most deserts?

(Tropical climate)

In which climate can you find ice and snow all year round?

(Polar climate)

In which climate does most of the world's population live?

(Temperate climate)

In which climate does the sun barely appear during the winter?

(Polar climate)

In which climate might you find an igloo?

(Polar climate)

What kind of climate does Antarctica have?

(Polar climate)

What kind of climate does Hawaii have?

(Tropical climate)

What kinds of climate does Mexico have?

(Tropical and temperate climates)

What kinds of climate does Canada have?

(Temperate and polar climate)

What kind of climate does most of the United States have?

(Temperate climate)

What kinds of climate does South America have?

(Tropical and temperate climates)

Which climate gets a lot of heavy rainfall?

(Tropical climate)

Which climate gets warm summers and cool winters?

(Temperate climate)

Great Map Games Scholastic Professional Books

AROUND THE WORLD

What kind of weather can you find in a polar climate?

(Cold, with lots of snow)

What kind of weather can you find in a tropical climate?

(Hot, rainy, and humid)

Where are you more likely to find tropical rain forests—North America or South America?

(South America)

If you were visiting Antarctica, would you bring a fur-lined jacket or a bathing suit?

(A fur-lined jacket)

Why is it so cold in the polar climate?

(It's far away from the equator and doesn't get direct rays from the sun.)

REFUELING.
Skip a turn.

LOST LUGGAGE!
Go back
3 spaces.

FOGGED IN!
Skip a turn.

MISSED FLIGHT!
Skip a turn.

JET LAG!
Go back
2 spaces.

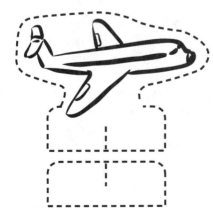

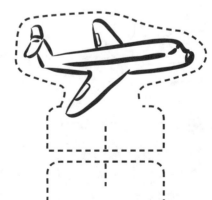

Assemble markers as shown.

RACE TO THE SUMMIT!

On the Earth's surface, *highlands*, such as mountains and hills, soar above *lowlands*, like plains and valleys. Maps often show *elevation*, or the height of a place, using different-color bands for each level. Use your knowledge of elevation to scale the top of a mountain!

SKILL

Understand elevation

PLAYERS

2

MATERIALS

- ✪ Race to the Summit! Game Board
- ✪ Summit Question Cards
- ✪ Pencil for each player

Before You Play

Photocopy the game board on oak tag and use a craft knife to cut along the dotted line. Fold the mountain along the solid line. Use tape to secure the game-board base to the table.

EXTENSION

Do research and make up your own mountain fact cards. Have another person do the same and take turns asking each other your questions.

HOW TO PLAY

1. Shuffle the Summit Question Cards and place them facedown in a pile within easy reach of both players. Each player gets a pencil.

2. Play starts at Sea Level. To move up a level, correctly answer questions from the Summit Question Cards. Take turns drawing a card from the pile and asking each other questions. If you answer a question correctly, write your initials on a flag at the next-higher level. (The first flags are at 2,500 feet.) If not, the other player reads aloud the correct answer and returns the card to the bottom of the pile. The other player takes a turn.

3. If you draw a Rock Slide card, move down one level by erasing your initials from your flag at the current level. If you draw an Avalanche card, erase your initials from all your flags and start again at Sea Level.

4. The first player to reach the summit (25,000 ft) wins.

Great Map Games Scholastic Professional Books

RACE TO THE SUMMIT!

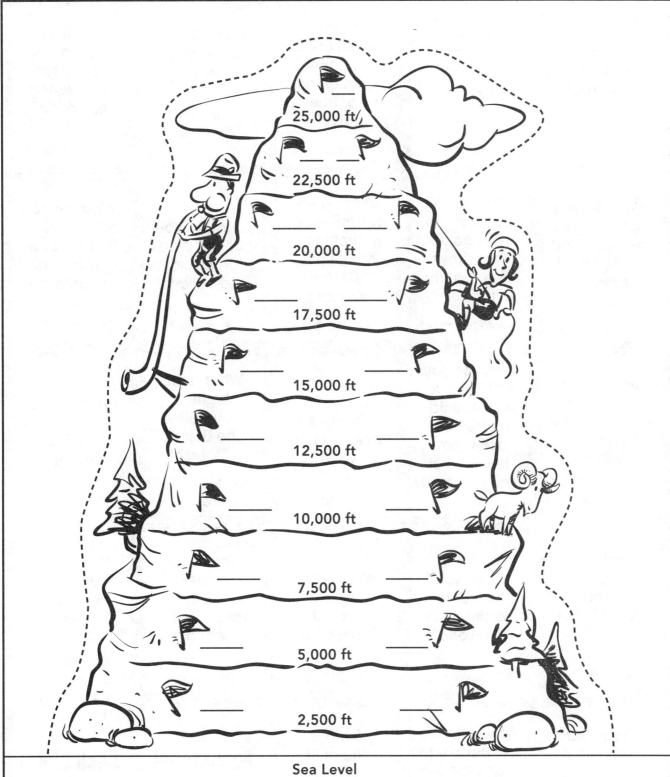

25,000 ft

22,500 ft

20,000 ft

17,500 ft

15,000 ft

12,500 ft

10,000 ft

7,500 ft

5,000 ft

2,500 ft

Sea Level

RACE TO THE SUMMIT!

What does elevation measure?

(The height of a place)

What is another word for elevation?

(Altitude)

Colors are often used to show elevation on a map. True or false?

(True)

What does a relief map show?

(Different elevations of land)

What is the starting point for measuring elevation?

(Sea level)

What do you call lines that connect land of the same height?

(Contour lines)

If a mountain is very steep, are its contour lines drawn close together or far apart?

(Close together)

What do you call tall areas such as mountains, hills, and mesas?

(Highlands)

What do you call flat areas such as plains and valleys?

(Lowlands)

What do you call low areas that separate hills and mountains?

(Valleys)

Does it get warmer or colder as you climb up a mountain?

(Colder)

What do you call the level on a mountain where trees don't grow because of wind and cold?

(Tree line)

What is the highest country in the world?

(Nepal)

What is the highest mountain in the United States?

(Mt. McKinley, also known as Denali)

What is the highest mountain in the world?

(Mt. Everest)

What is the highest mountain range in the world?

(The Himalaya)

What is the highest volcanic mountain in the world?

(Mt. Kilimanjaro)

What is the highest waterfall in the world?

(Angel Falls)

What is the longest mountain range in the world?

(The Andes)

What is the deepest place in the ocean?

(The Mariana Trench)

The ocean floor is flat and has no mountains. True or false?

(False)

Who were the first people to reach the top of Mt. Everest?

(Sir Edmund Hillary and Tenzing Norgay)

Earth is the only planet with mountains. True or false?

(False)

Avalanche!

Go back to sea level.

Rock Slide!

Go back one level.

Great Map Games Scholastic Professional Books

GOT THE TIME?

Did you know that while people are eating lunch in New York, folks in Alaska are just waking up? Because of the Earth's rotation, the sun rises and sets in different places at different times. Can you figure out the correct standard time in different places in the U.S.?

SKILL

Use a map key to compute differences in time zones

PLAYERS

Up to 4

MATERIALS

- Got the Time? Game Board
- Clock and Hands for each player
- 30 Time Pieces
- Time Cards

Before You Play:

Photocopy the Clocks and Hands and glue them to oak tag, then cut them out. Use a sharp pencil to poke a hole through the center of each Clock and the ends of the Hands. Then, assemble the Clocks and Hands using paper fasteners, as shown.

EXTENSION

Find a time-zone world map and choose a country in a different time zone. What would a person in that country be doing at the same time you're having lunch here?

HOW TO PLAY

1. Each player receives a Clock and three Time Pieces. Keep the leftover Time Pieces in a pile nearby. Shuffle the Time Cards and stack them facedown in a pile.

2. Take turns reading aloud a Time Card to the other players. When you read a card, set your Clock to the underlined time and show your Clock to the other players. The others must decide what time to set their Clocks based on the question asked. For example, if a card reads, "It is <u>4:00 P.M.</u> in New Jersey. What time is it in Missouri?" set your Clock to 4:00. The other players must set their Clocks to Missouri's time. Use the game board for reference. Check the players' Clocks against the correct time written at the bottom of the Time Card. Each player who gets the correct time takes one Time Piece from the pile. Players with the wrong time must put one of their Time Pieces in the pile. Put the card in a discard pile. The next player takes a turn reading a card.

3. Play continues until all Time Cards have been read. The player with the most Time Pieces wins.

GOT THE TIME?

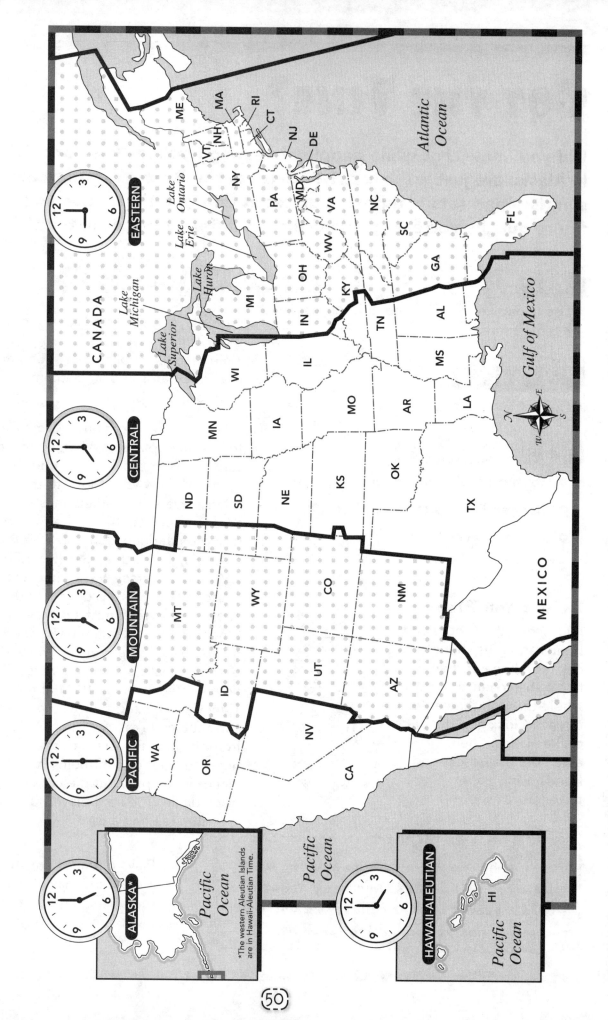

EASTERN

CENTRAL

MOUNTAIN

PACIFIC

ALASKA*

HAWAII-ALEUTIAN

CANADA

MEXICO

Atlantic Ocean

Gulf of Mexico

Pacific Ocean

Pacific Ocean

Pacific Ocean

ME
VT
NH
MA
RI
CT
NY
NJ
DE
PA
MD
VA
WV
NC
SC
GA
FL
OH
KY
TN
AL
MS
IN
IL
MI
WI
MN
IA
MO
AR
LA
ND
SD
NE
KS
OK
TX
MT
WY
CO
NM
ID
UT
AZ
NV
CA
OR
WA
HI

Lake Ontario
Lake Erie
Lake Huron
Lake Michigan
Lake Superior

*The western Aleutian Islands are in Hawaii-Aleutian Time.

(50)

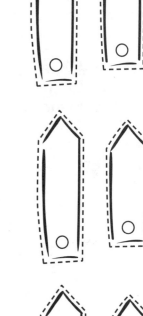

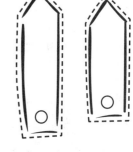

GOT THE TIME?

It's 12:00 P.M. in Colorado. What time is it in North Carolina?

(2:00 A.M.)

It's 1:00 A.M. in West Virginia. What time is it in New Mexico?

(11:00 P.M.)

It's 2:00 A.M. in Delaware. What time is it in Michigan?

(2:00 A.M.)

It's 3:00 A.M. in Texas. What time is it in California?

(1:00 A.M.)

It's 4:00 A.M. in Montana. What time is it in Maine?

(6:00 A.M.)

It's 6:00 A.M. in Missouri. What time is it in Vermont?

(7:00 A.M.)

It's 9:00 A.M. in Connecticut. What time is it in Louisiana?

(8:00 A.M.)

It's 6:00 A.M. in Hawaii. What time is it in Alabama?

(10:00 A.M.)

It's 10:00 A.M. in Wyoming. What time is it in Maryland?

(12:00 noon)

It's 12:00 P.M. in Alaska. What time is it in Georgia?

(4:00 A.M.)

It's 1:00 P.M. in Wisconsin. What time is it in Texas?

(1:00 P.M.)

It's 2:00 P.M. in Mississippi. What time is it in South Carolina?

(3:00 P.M.)

It's 4:00 P.M. in Oklahoma. What time is it in Oregon?

(2:00 P.M.)

It's 5:00 P.M. in New York. What time is it in Utah?

(3:00 P.M.)

It's 6:00 P.M. in Ohio. What time is it in Nevada?

(3:00 P.M.)

It's 8:00 P.M. in Arizona. What time is it in Pennsylvania?

(10:00 P.M.)

Great Map Games Scholastic Professional Books

RED, WHITE, AND BLUE

There are 50 states in the United States. Can you identify them based on their capitals?

SKILL

Use a political map of the United States to identify state capitals and abbreviations

PLAYERS

2

MATERIALS

- Red, White, and Blue Game Board
- Red and Blue Crayons
- State Capital Cards

HOW TO PLAY

1. Shuffle the State Capital Cards and place them facedown in a pile. Each player chooses a red or blue crayon.

2. Take turns drawing a card. Read the statement on the card to each other. If you can correctly identify the state and locate it on the game board, color the state with your crayon. If not, leave the state uncolored. The other player puts the card in a discard pile and takes a turn.

3. Play continues until all cards have been drawn. Count the number of states each player has colored. The person with the most states wins.

EXTENSION

Research one of the states on the map and design a travel poster that will make people want to come and visit.

RED, WHITE, AND BLUE

United States of America

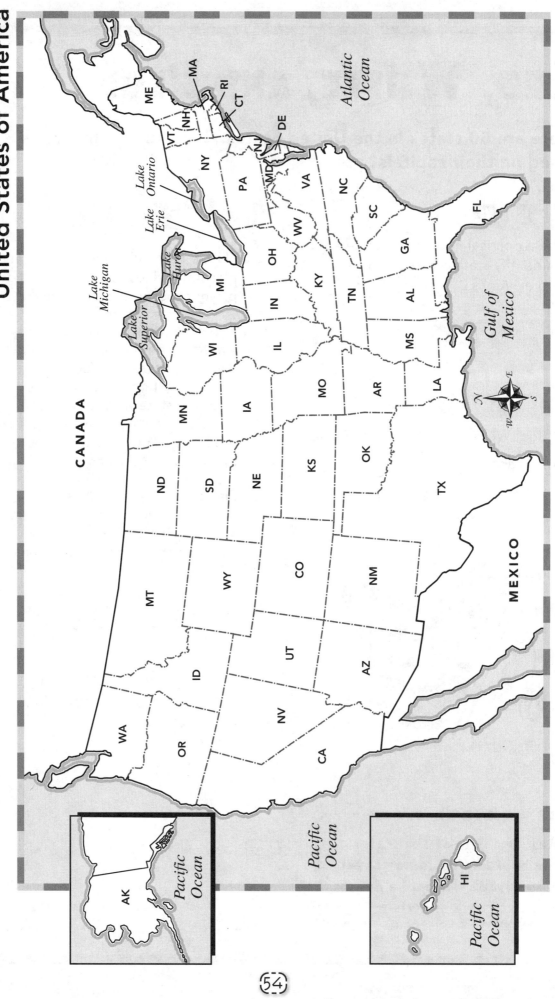

CANADA

MEXICO

Atlantic Ocean

Gulf of Mexico

Pacific Ocean

Pacific Ocean

Pacific Ocean

Lake Ontario
Lake Erie
Lake Huron
Lake Michigan
Lake Superior

ME
MA
NH
VT
RI
CT
NY
PA
NJ
MD
DE
VA
WV
OH
NC
SC
GA
FL
KY
TN
AL
IN
MS
IL
MI
WI
LA
AR
MO
IA
MN
OK
KS
TX
NE
SD
ND
CO
NM
WY
MT
UT
AZ
NV
ID
OR
WA
CA
AK
HI

Number Red _____

Number Blue _____

Great Map Games Scholastic Professional Books

RED, WHITE, AND BLUE

The 1st state; its capital is Dover.	The 2nd state; its capital is Harrisburg.	The 3rd state; its capital is Trenton.	The 4th state; its capital is Atlanta.	The 5th state; its capital is Hartford.
(Delaware)	(Pennsylvania)	(New Jersey)	(Georgia)	(Connecticut)
The 6th state; its capital is Boston.	The 7th state; its capital is Annapolis.	The 8th state; its capital is Columbia.	The 9th state; its capital is Concord.	The 10th state; its capital is Richmond.
(Massachusetts)	(Maryland)	(South Carolina)	(New Hampshire)	(Virginia)
The 11th state; its capital is Albany.	The 12th state; its capital is Raleigh.	The 13th state; its capital is Providence.	The 14th state; its capital is Montpelier.	The 15th state; its capital is Frankfort.
(New York)	(North Carolina)	(Rhode Island)	(Vermont)	(Kentucky)
The 16th state; its capital is Nashville.	The 17th state; its capital is Columbus.	The 18th state; its capital is Baton Rouge.	The 19th state; its capital is Indianapolis.	The 20th state; its capital is Jackson.
(Tennessee)	(Ohio)	(Louisiana)	(Indiana)	(Mississippi)
The 21st state; its capital is Springfield.	The 22nd state; its capital is Montgomery.	The 23rd state; its capital is Augusta.	The 24th state; its capital is Jefferson City.	The 25th state; its capital is Little Rock.
(Illinois)	(Alabama)	(Maine)	(Missouri)	(Arkansas)

RED, WHITE, AND BLUE

The 26th state; its capital is Lansing.	The 27th state; its capital is Tallahassee.	The 28th state; its capital is Austin.	The 29th state; its capital is Des Moines.	The 30th state; its capital is Madison.
(Michigan)	(Florida)	(Texas)	(Iowa)	(Wisconsin)
The 31st state; its capital is Sacramento.	The 32nd state; its capital is St. Paul.	The 33rd state; its capital is Salem.	The 34th state; its capital is Topeka.	The 35th state; its capital is Charleston.
(California)	(Minnesota)	(Oregon)	(Kansas)	(West Virginia)
The 36th state; its capital is Carson City.	The 37th state; its capital is Lincoln.	The 38th state; its capital is Denver.	The 39th state; its capital is Bismarck.	The 40th state; its capital is Pierre.
(Nevada)	(Nebraska)	(Colorado)	(North Dakota)	(South Dakota)
The 41st state; its capital is Helena.	The 42nd state; its capital is Olympia.	The 43rd state; its capital is Boise.	The 44th state; its capital is Cheyenne.	The 45th state; its capital is Salt Lake City.
(Montana)	(Washington)	(Idaho)	(Wyoming)	(Utah)
The 46th state; its capital is Oklahoma City.	The 47th state; its capital is Santa Fe.	The 48th state; its capital is Phoenix.	The 49th state; its capital is Juneau.	The 50th state; its capital is Honolulu.
(Oklahoma)	(New Mexico)	(Arizona)	(Alaska)	(Hawaii)

Great Map Games Scholastic Professional Books

BIRDS OF A FEATHER

Like many birds, sandhill cranes *migrate*, or travel south for the winter. These long-necked birds travel thousands of miles, from Canada, across the United States, and finally to Mexico. How many sandhill cranes can you help cross the borders?

SKILL

Identify borders

PLAYERS

2

MATERIALS

- Birds-of-a-Feather Game Board
- 4 Sandhill Crane Markers for each player
- Birds-of-a-Feather Question Cards

HOW TO PLAY

1. Take a close look at the game board. Notice the lines that separate countries, states, and provinces. This line ——— separates one country from another. This line –·–·–·– separates states or provinces within a country. A large body of water or a mountain range can also serve as a border.

2. Shuffle the Birds-of-a-Feather Question Cards and put them facedown in a stack. Each player takes four Sandhill Cranes and places them on Canada.

3. Take turns drawing a card and asking each other a question. If you answer the question correctly, move one Sandhill Crane south to the next country. If not, the other player reads aloud the correct answer and returns the card to the bottom of the pile. The other player takes a turn.

4. The first player to move all his or her Cranes to Mexico wins.

EXTENSION

Winter is over! If you have cards left over, keep playing the game—only this time, get your birds back to Canada!

U. S.

Yukon
Territory

Northwest
Territories

Nunavut

British
Columbia

CANADA

Newfoundland

Alberta

Saskatchewan

Manitoba

Ontario

Quebec

Nova
Scotia

New Brunswick

UNITED STATES

Pacific
Ocean

Atlantic
Ocean

Gulf of
Mexico

N
W   E
S

MEXICO

BELIZE

HONDURAS

GUATEMALA

NICARAGUA

EL SALVADOR

PANAMA

COSTA RICA

MAP KEY

—— National boundary

–··– State, provincial, or
territorial boundary

Great Map Games Scholastic Professional Books

BIRDS OF A FEATHER

What is a border? (A boundary line on a map that separates places under different governments)	What country is located above the United States' northern border? (Canada)	What body of water borders the United States on the west? (The Pacific Ocean)	What body of water borders the United States on the east? (The Atlantic Ocean)
What country borders the United States in the south? (Mexico)	What do you call small areas that make up a country? (States, provinces, or territories)	What do you call smaller areas that make up a state? (Counties)	How many states make up the United States? (50)
Which four U.S. states border Mexico? (California, Arizona, New Mexico, and Texas)	Which U.S. state borders Canada's northwest corner? (Alaska)	Which two Canadian provinces border Ontario? (Manitoba and Quebec)	Which three states border California? (Oregon, Nevada, and Arizona)
What large bodies of water border Florida? (The Gulf of Mexico and the Atlantic Ocean)	What body of water is part of Mexico's eastern border? (The Gulf of Mexico)	What three countries border Mexico? (The United States, Guatemala, and Belize)	In what country can you find the Northwest Territories? (Canada)
Which two U.S. states border Manitoba? (North Dakota and Minnesota)	What two Canadian provinces border Maine? (New Brunswick and Quebec)	What two bodies of water border Wisconsin? (Lake Superior and Lake Michigan)	What continent are Canada, the United States, and Mexico part of? (North America)

BIRDS OF A FEATHER

Assemble markers as shown.

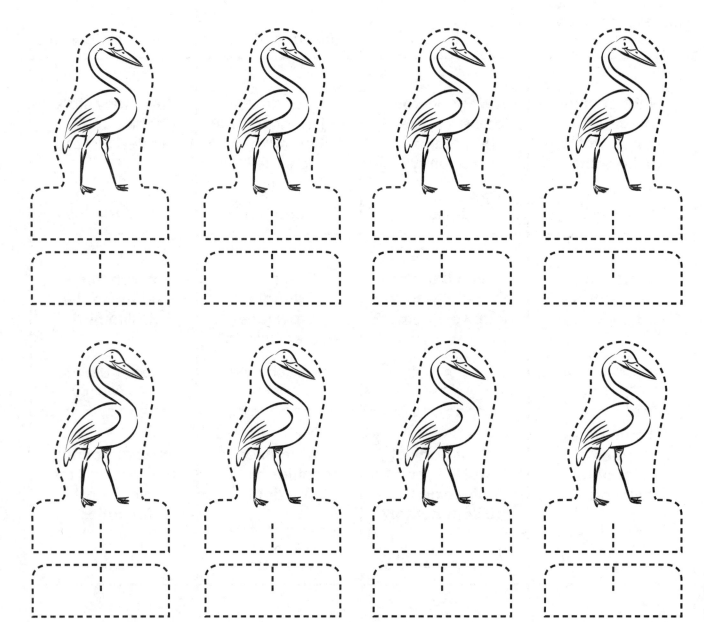

Great Map Games Scholastic Professional Books

COUNTRY MATCH-UPS

Do you know where the Eiffel Tower is? What about the Matterhorn? Our world has many interesting countries to explore and visit. See how many facts you can learn about some of them!

SKILL

Identify and explore countries

PLAYERS

2

MATERIALS

❂ Country Match-up Playing Cards

HOW TO PLAY

1. Shuffle the Country Match-up Playing Cards and deal each player seven cards. Stack the remaining cards facedown. Take the top card and place it faceup next to the pile. This will be the discard pile.

2. Look at your cards and pair them up. In a matching pair, one card will show the outline of a country, and the other will display the country's flag and list interesting facts about the place. Put matching pairs faceup on the table.

3. You may do one of three things:

❂ Ask the other player for a card that you need to make a match.

❂ Take the top card from the discard pile.

❂ If the other player doesn't have a matching card and you don't want a card from the discard pile, draw a new card from the card stack.

Each time you take a card, put one of your cards in the discard pile.

4. Play ends when one player runs out of cards. Count up your card pairs. The player with the most matching pairs wins.

VARIATION

Use the Country Match-up cards to play Concentration. Shuffle the cards and lay them facedown in four rows. Take turns flipping over two cards. If you get two matching cards, keep the cards. When no more cards are left, the person with the most cards wins.

COUNTRY MATCH-UPS

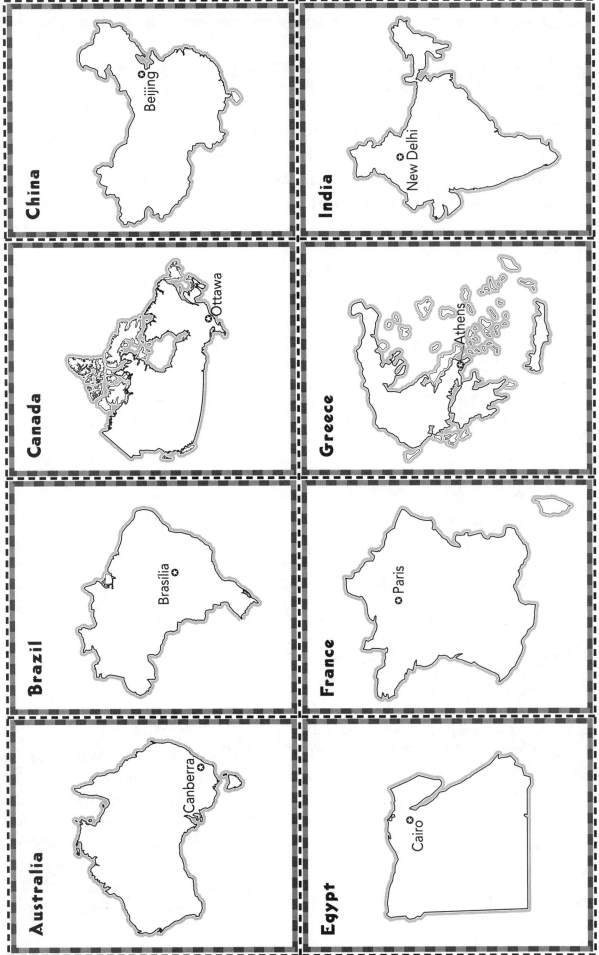

Australia — Canberra

Brazil — Brasília

Canada — Ottawa

China — Beijing

Egypt — Cairo

France — Paris

Greece — Athens

India — New Delhi

COUNTRY MATCH-UPS

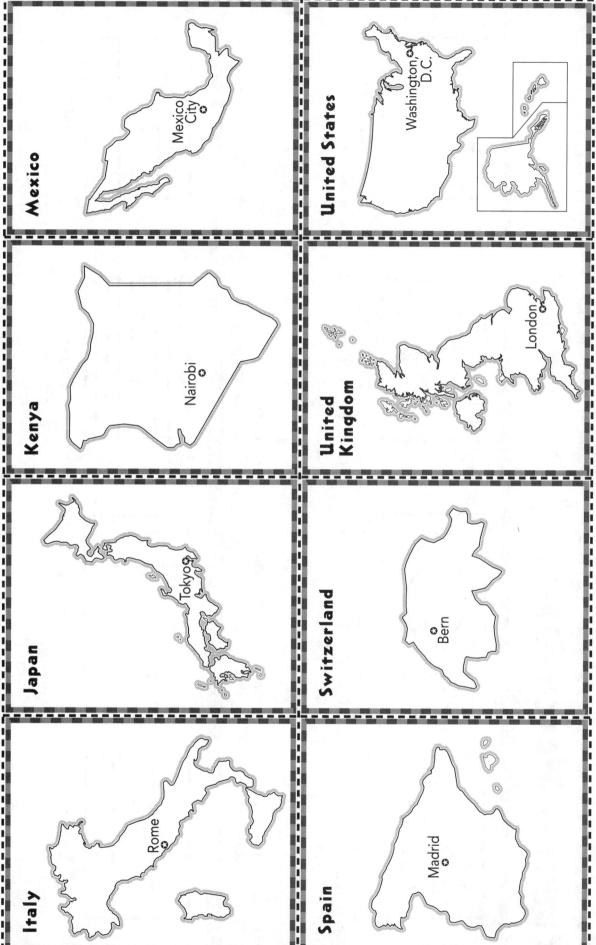

Mexico — Mexico City

United States — Washington, D.C.

Kenya — Nairobi

United Kingdom — London

Japan — Tokyo

Switzerland — Bern

Italy — Rome

Spain — Madrid

Great Map Games Scholastic Professional Books

COUNTRY MATCH-UPS

China

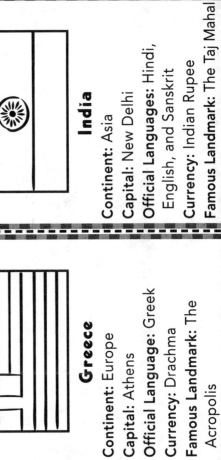

Continent: Asia
Capital: Beijing
Official Language: Mandarin
Currency: Yuan
Famous Landmark: The Great Wall

India

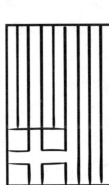

Continent: Asia
Capital: New Delhi
Official Languages: Hindi, English, and Sanskrit
Currency: Indian Rupee
Famous Landmark: The Taj Mahal

Canada

Continent: North America
Capital: Ottawa
Official Languages: English and French
Currency: Canadian Dollar
Famous Landmark: Niagara Falls

Greece

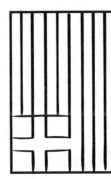

Continent: Europe
Capital: Athens
Official Language: Greek
Currency: Drachma
Famous Landmark: The Acropolis

Brazil

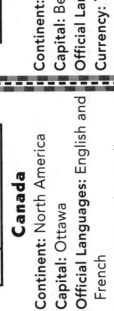

Continent: South America
Capital: Brasília
Official Language: Portuguese
Currency: Cruzeiro Real
Famous Landmark: Amazon River

France

Continent: Europe
Capital: Paris
Official Language: French
Currency: Franc and Euro
Famous Landmark: The Eiffel Tower

Australia

Continent: Australia
Capital: Canberra
Official Language: English
Currency: Australian Dollar
Famous Landmark: Sydney Opera House

Egypt

Continent: Africa
Capital: Cairo
Official Language: Arabic
Currency: Egyptian Pound
Famous Landmark: The Great Pyramids

Great Map Games Scholastic Professional Books

COUNTRY MATCH-UPS

Mexico

Continent: North America
Capital: Mexico City
Official Language: Spanish
Currency: Mexican Peso
Famous Landmark: Aztec and Maya Ruins

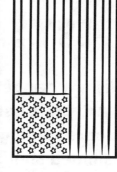

United States

Continent: North America
Capital: Washington, D.C.
Language: English
Currency: U.S. Dollar
Famous Landmark: The Statue of Liberty

Kenya

Continent: Africa
Capital: Nairobi
Official Languages: Swahili and English
Currency: Kenya Shilling
Famous Landmark: Amboseli National Park

United Kingdom

Continent: Europe
Capital: London
Language: English
Currency: Pound Sterling
Famous Landmark: Big Ben

Japan

Continent: Asia
Capital: Tokyo
Official Language: Japanese
Currency: Yen
Famous Landmark: Mt. Fuji

Switzerland

Continent: Europe
Capital: Bern
Official Languages: German, French, and Italian
Currency: Swiss Franc
Famous Landmark: The Matterhorn

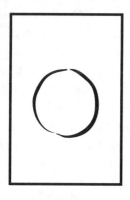

Italy

Continent: Europe
Capital: Rome
Official Language: Italian
Currency: Lira and Euro
Famous Landmark: The Colosseum

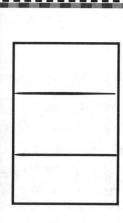

Spain

Continent: Europe
Capital: Madrid
Official Language: Castilian Spanish
Currency: Peseta and Euro
Famous Landmark: Port of Barcelona

ART HEIST!

Help! Alarm bells are clanging at the City Museum of Art. Master criminal Art Craft has tried to snatch a priceless work of art. Luckily, all doors leading to and from the different galleries automatically slammed shut the moment the alarm went off. The thief has nowhere to go. But where's Craft? Gather clues to nab the crook!

SKILL

Read a room layout

PLAYERS

Up to 4, plus a Curator

MATERIALS

- Art Heist Game Board
- Magnifying Glass Marker for each player
- Clue Cards
- Thief Card
- Number Cube

HOW TO PLAY

1. Stack the Clue Cards facedown near the board. Each player gets a Magnifying Glass marker and places it on START. The Curator keeps the Thief Card.

2. Take turns rolling the number cube to move around the board clockwise. If you land on a Clue space, pick a card, read the clue quietly, then return the card to the bottom of the pile. You can then either guess which gallery the thief is in or continue to play. If you choose to guess the thief's hideout, move your Magnifying Glass to that room. The Curator will tell you whether or not you're correct. If you guess correctly, you win. If not, you're out of the game.

3. Play continues until a player has guessed correctly in which gallery the thief is hiding.

EXTENSION

Create your own museum! Think of what kind of museum you'd have and what you'd put in it. Then make a floor plan to help visitors find their way around.

Great Map Games Scholastic Professional Books

Art Heist!

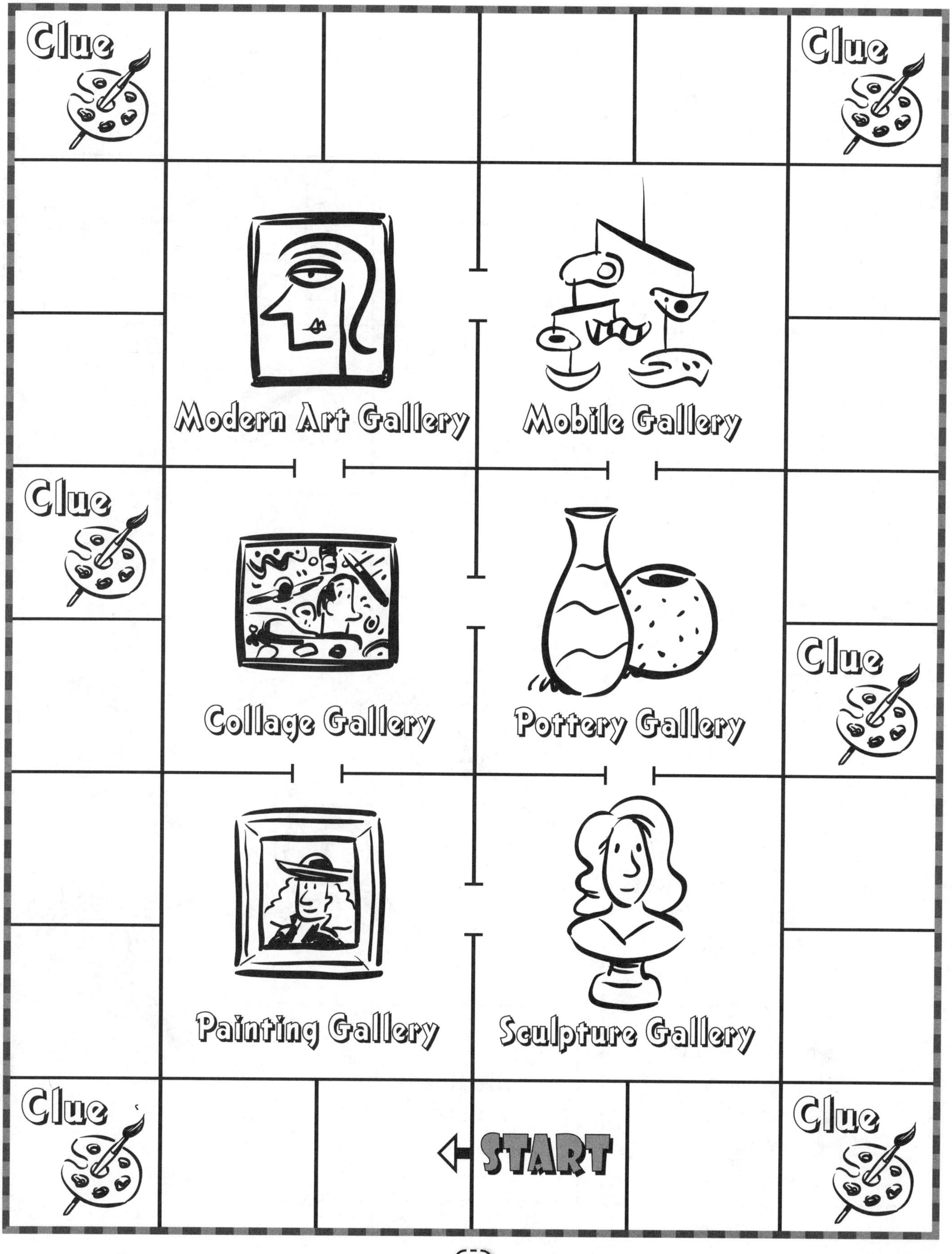
Clue
Clue
Modern Art Gallery
Mobile Gallery
Clue
Collage Gallery
Pottery Gallery
Clue
Painting Gallery
Sculpture Gallery
Clue
START
Clue

Great Map Games Scholastic Professional Books

ART HEIST!

Next door to the thief's hideout, you'll find many statues.

No door leads directly from the Modern Art Gallery to the room where the thief is hiding.

The thief is not in the Collage Gallery.

Three doors lead to the gallery where the thief is hiding.

Next door to the thief's hideout, you'll find lots of artwork hanging from the ceiling.

The thief is not in the gallery where you'll find paintings.

Clue Cards

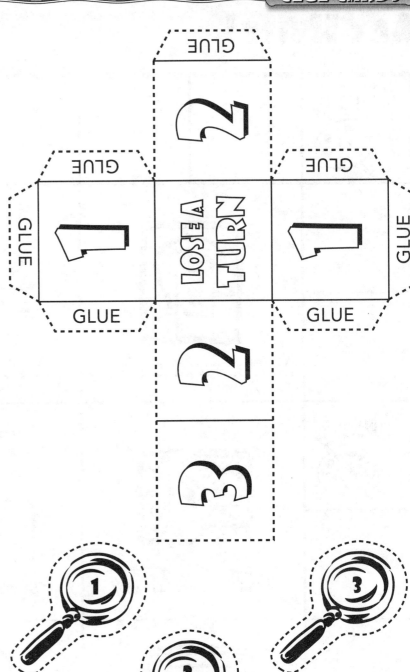

The thief is in the Pottery Gallery.

Thief Card

TRACK THOSE CROOKS!

Calling all cars! Crime is breaking out everywhere in downtown Pokey City. Use your wits and map skills to track down these criminals.

SKILL

Read a street map

PLAYERS

Up to 3 players

MATERIALS

❂ Track Those Crooks! Game Board

❂ 5 Tickets per player

❂ Dispatcher Cards

HOW TO PLAY

1. Shuffle the Dispatcher Cards and place them facedown in a stack.

2. Take turns drawing Dispatcher Cards and asking each other questions. Answer a question by finding either the location of or directions to the crime scene on the game board. If you answer correctly, turn in one of your tickets to the Police Station. Otherwise, keep the ticket. The other player takes a turn.

3. The first player to get rid of all his or her tickets wins.

Police Station

EXTENSION

Draw a street map of your school and your house. Then write directions on how to get to your house from school. Invite a friend to "drive" the route using a crayon.

TRACK THOSE CROOKS!

DOWNTOWN POKEY CITY

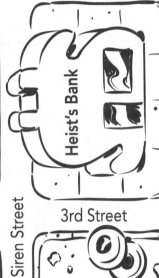
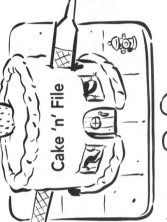
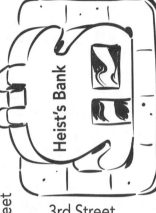

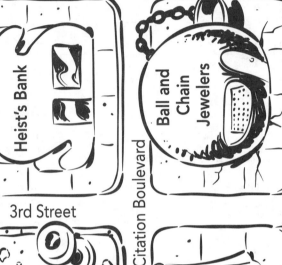

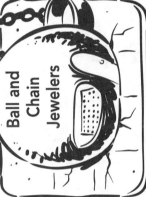

Crime Busters Book Store

Hoodlum's Park

Jailbird Café

Parking Lot

4th Street

Cake 'n' File

Heist's Bank

Ball and Chain Jewelers

Siren Street

3rd Street

Citation Boulevard

Violation Road

Arresting Fashions Clothing Store

Vacant Lot

Squealers Restaurant

2nd Street

Police Station

Whistle Blowers Music Store

Stool Pigeons Pet Store

City Jail

1st Street

Great Map Games Scholastic Professional Books

TRACK THOSE CROOKS!

A purse snatcher is hanging out on the northwest corner of Citation Boulevard and 4th Street. Where should you go?

(Heist's Bank)

Jail break! You're at Jailbird Café. What's the quickest route to the City Jail?

(South on 4th Street then west on Violation Road)

Pickpocket alert at the northeast corner of 3rd Street and Violation Road. Where should you go?

(Ball and Chain Jewelers)

Mad dog at Hoodlum's Park! You're at the Police Station. What is the quickest route to the park?

(East on Siren Street, then south on 4th Street)

Disorderly conduct at the southeast corner of Citation Boulevard and 4th Street. Where should you go?

(Jailbird Café)

You follow a speeding car to Siren Street. The car turns south onto 3rd Street and parks illegally at the northwest corner of 3rd and Violation Road. Where are you?

(Squealers Restaurant)

Suspicious characters have been reported loitering at the southwest corner of Siren Street and 3rd Street. Where should you go?

(The Vacant Lot)

Shoplifter reported at Crime Busters Book Store! You're at the City Jail. What is the quickest route to the store?

(East on Violation Road, then north on 4th Street)

Bank robbery! You chase the suspects west on Citation Boulevard and then north on 2nd Street. You arrest them on the southwest corner of Siren Street and 2nd Street. Where are you?

(Whistle Blowers Music Store)

A litterbug throws trash in front of the Jailbird Café. He walks north on 4th Street and then turns west on Siren Street. He ducks into a store on the northwest corner of Siren and 3rd Streets. Where do you go?

(Arresting Fashions)

A jaywalker crosses from the northwest corner of Siren Street and 4th Street to the southeast corner. Where do you nab him?

(In Hoodlum's Park)

A rare snake was stolen from Stool Pigeons Pet Store. A suspect matching the thief's description is seen at the northeast corner of Violation Road and 4th Street. Where should you go?

(Jailbird Café)

Someone has run a red light at the intersection of 4th Street and Siren. You're at the Police Station. In which direction will you go?

(East)

A broken-down car is blocking the intersection of 2nd Street and Violation Road. You're at the Police Station. In which direction will you go?

(South)

There's an accident at the intersection of 3rd Street and Citation Boulevard. You're at the Police Station. In which direction will you go?

(East, then south, or south, then east)

TRACK THOSE CROOKS!

Someone has locked their keys in their car in the Parking Lot. You're at Crime Busters Book Store. In which direction will you go?

(South)

A car has been stolen! It was last seen heading north on 4th Street. You're at the City Jail. What's the quickest way to follow that car?

(Go east on Violation Road and north on 4th Street)

You finished setting up a roadblock at the intersection of 4th Street and Citation Boulevard. It's lunch time. Where's the closest place to get something to eat?

(Jailbird Café)

Great Map Games Scholastic Professional Books

TOUR GUIDE

Take a tour of our nation's capital, Washington, D.C. Load up your Tour Bus with tourists and show them the sights!

SKILL

Read a landmark map

PLAYERS

2

MATERIALS

- ✪ Tour Guide Game Board
- ✪ Tour Bus for each player
- ✪ 12 Passengers (pennies)
- ✪ Sightseeing Cards

HOW TO PLAY

1. Shuffle the Sightseeing Cards and place them facedown in a stack. Each player gets a Tour Bus.

2. Take turns drawing a Sightseeing Card and asking each other questions about Washington's landmarks. Use the game board for reference. If you answer correctly, add a passenger to your bus. If not, don't take on a passenger. The other player takes a turn.

3. The first person to fill up a bus with passengers wins.

VARIATION

Load your bus with passengers. Take turns reading each other question cards. If you have the correct answer, drop your passenger off at that location. The first person to unload all six passengers wins.

TOUR GUIDE

Washington, D.C.

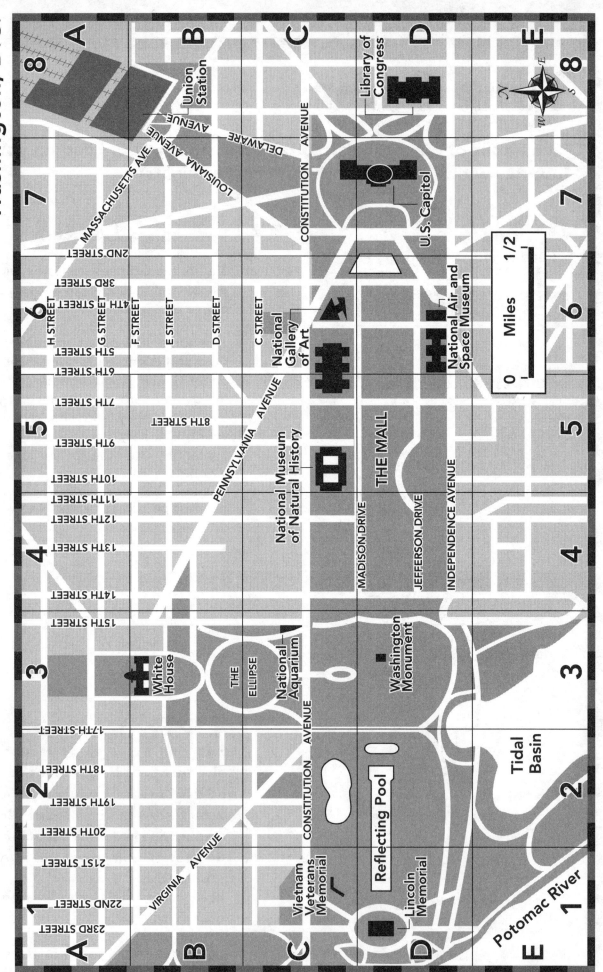

Union Station

Library of Congress

U.S. Capitol

CONSTITUTION AVENUE

DELAWARE AVENUE

LOUISIANA AVENUE

MASSACHUSETTS AVE.

2ND STREET
3RD STREET
4TH STREET
5TH STREET
6TH STREET
7TH STREET
8TH STREET
9TH STREET
10TH STREET
11TH STREET
12TH STREET
13TH STREET
14TH STREET
15TH STREET
17TH STREET
18TH STREET
19TH STREET
20TH STREET
21ST STREET
22ND STREET
23RD STREET

H STREET
G STREET
F STREET
E STREET
D STREET
C STREET

National Gallery of Art

National Air and Space Museum

National Museum of Natural History

PENNSYLVANIA AVENUE

THE MALL

MADISON DRIVE
JEFFERSON DRIVE
INDEPENDENCE AVENUE

Washington Monument

White House

THE ELLIPSE

National Aquarium

CONSTITUTION AVENUE

VIRGINIA AVENUE

Reflecting Pool

Vietnam Veterans Memorial

Lincoln Memorial

Tidal Basin

Potomac River

Miles
0   1/2

A 8 B C D E 8
7   7
6   6
5   5
4   4
3   3
2   2
A 1 B C D E 1

N
W E
S

Great Map Games Scholastic Professional Books

TOUR GUIDE

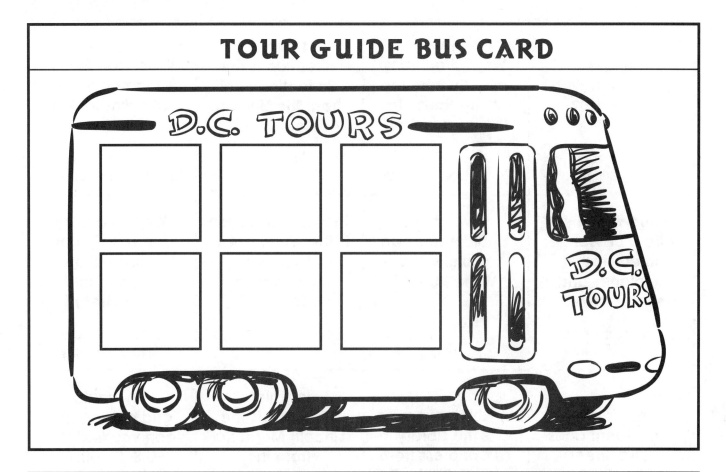

TOUR GUIDE BUS CARD

TOUR GUIDE BUS CARD

TOUR GUIDE

Where could you take a passenger who loves fish? (The National Aquarium)	What street runs directly from the White House to the U.S. Capitol? (Pennsylvania Avenue)	In what direction is the Reflecting Pool from the Lincoln Memorial? (East)	Which landmark is located in grid coordinate D8? (The Library of Congress)
Where would you take a passenger interested in airplanes and space travel? (The National Air and Space Museum)	In what grid coordinates can you find the White House? (B3)	In which direction is the White House from the Washington Monument? (North)	What is across the street from Constitution Avenue and 10th Street? (The National Museum of Natural History)
What famous monument does 23rd Street lead to? (The Lincoln Memorial)	In which direction is the Library of Congress from Union Station? (South)	In which direction is the Lincoln Memorial from the White House? (Southwest)	In what grid coordinate can you find the U.S. Capitol Building? (D7)
Where could you take a passenger who loves books? (The Library of Congress)	Which famous landmark is at the eastern end of the Mall? (The U.S. Capitol)	Which famous landmark is at the western end of the Mall? (The Lincoln Memorial)	Where would be a good place to take someone interested in dinosaur bones and fossils? (The National Museum of Natural History)
Which street runs in front of the National Air and Space Museum? (Independence Avenue)	Where would you take a passenger interested in seeing where Congress makes laws? (The U.S. Capitol)	You have passengers who want to see where the President lives. Where would you take them? (The White House)	What small body of water lies between the Lincoln Memorial and Washington Monument? (The Reflecting Pool)

Great Map Games Scholastic Professional Books

ROAD TRIP

Pack the car and grab the road map! We're driving to Yellowstone National Park! Road maps help you find the best roads to take, give you directions to follow, and tell you how far to drive. *Bon voyage!*

SKILL

Use a road map

PLAYERS

2 or more

MATERIALS

- Road Trip Game Board
- Number Cube
- Road Trip Question Cards
- Souvenir Card for each player
- Car Marker for each player

Geographically Speaking...

Study the map and key on the Road Trip game board. This map shows interstate highways and other major roads. The Highway Department assigns numbers to these roads—some roads may have more than one number.

The small number between two dots shows the distance in miles between those dots. To calculate the distance between two towns, add up the miles along that route. For example, say you want to know how many miles it is from Cheyenne to Lusk. Find Cheyenne and Lusk. Between the two towns, the numbers you'll find between dots are 84, 33, and 41: 84 + 33 + 41 = 158. The distance between Cheyenne and Lusk is about 158 miles.

HOW TO PLAY

1. Each player gets a Souvenir Card and a Car. Shuffle the Road Trip Question Cards and place them facedown in a stack. Put the Cars on Home.

2. Take turns rolling the number cube and moving clockwise around the game board. If you land on a Souvenir space, the player to your right draws a Road Trip Question Card from the stack and reads the question aloud. Use the game board for reference. If you answer correctly, "collect" the souvenir on the space by crossing it off your Souvenir Card. If you've already crossed out the souvenir on your card, wait for your next turn. The next player takes a turn.

3. Play continues until a player has collected all the souvenirs on a card and is first to return Home.

EXTENSION

Use a road map of your state. Pick a place you'd like to visit and write down the route you would take.

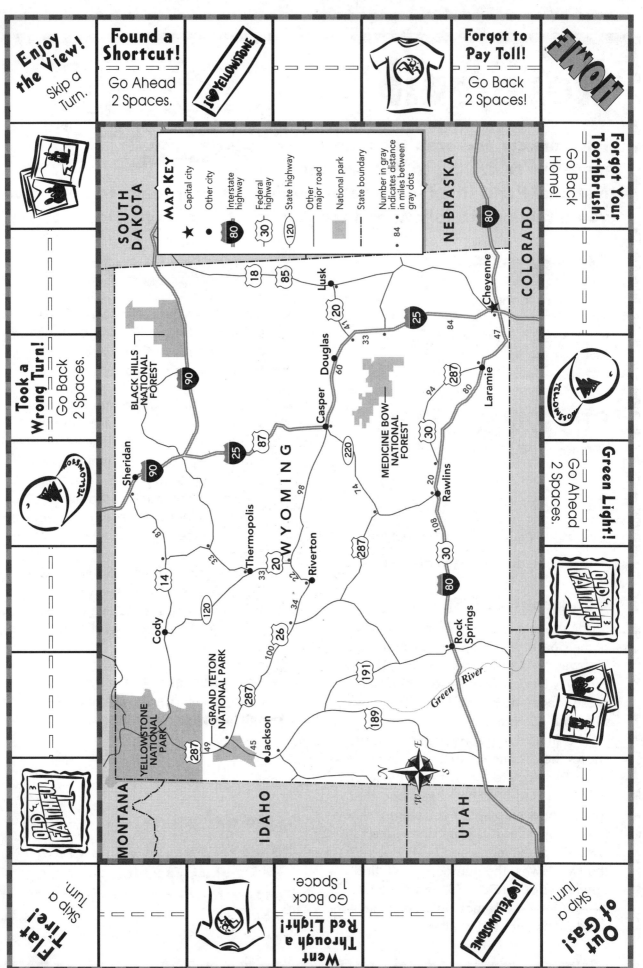

GAME BOARD

ROAD TRIP

Enjoy the View!
Skip a Turn.

Found a Shortcut!
Go Ahead 2 Spaces.

I ♥ YELLOWSTONE

Forgot to Pay Toll!
Go Back 2 Spaces!

HOME!

Took a Wrong Turn!
Go Back 2 Spaces.

YELLOWSTONE

Forgot Your Toothbrush!
Go Back Home!

YELLOWSTONE

Green Light!
Go Ahead 2 Spaces.

OLD FAITHFUL

OLD FAITHFUL

Flat Tire!
Skip a Turn.

Went Through a Red Light!
Go Back 1 Space.

Out of Gas!
Skip a Turn.

I ♥ YELLOWSTONE

MAP KEY

★ Capital city
● Other city
🛡80 Interstate highway
⬡30 Federal highway
⬭120 State highway
— Other major road
▨ National park
---- State boundary
● 84 Number in gray indicates distance in miles between gray dots

SOUTH DAKOTA

NEBRASKA

COLORADO

MONTANA

IDAHO

UTAH

WYOMING

BLACK HILLS NATIONAL FOREST

MEDICINE BOW NATIONAL FOREST

YELLOWSTONE NATIONAL PARK

GRAND TETON NATIONAL PARK

Sheridan
Cody
Thermopolis
Riverton
Jackson
Rock Springs
Rawlins
Laramie
Cheyenne
Casper
Douglas
Lusk

Green River

18 85 20 25 84 47 25 87 90 14 120 20 33 27 34 26 100 287 189 191 80 30 108 20 94 80 287 220 60 33 41 98 74 49 45

ROAD TRIP

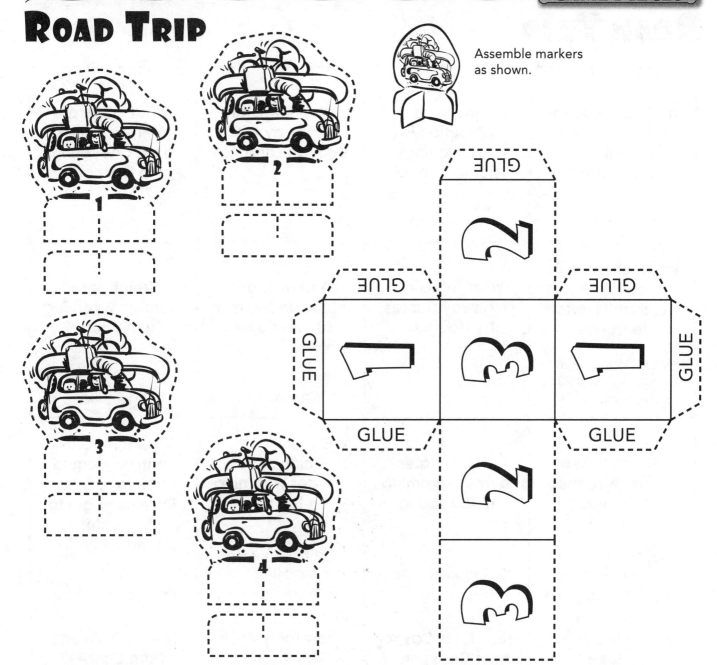

Assemble markers as shown.

GLUE

2

GLUE   GLUE

GLUE   1   3   1   GLUE

GLUE   GLUE

2

3

SOUVENIR CARD

T-Shirt	Bumper Sticker	Baseball Hat	Postcard	Snapshots

I ♥ YELLOWSTONE

YELLOWSTONE

OLD FAITHFUL

ROAD TRIP

In which direction is Yellowstone National Park from Cody? (West)	In which direction is Rock Springs from Casper? (Southwest)	What interstate highway runs through Laramie? (80)	What interstate highway goes from Cheyenne to Casper? (25)
What route would you take to get from Riverton to Cody? (Federal Highway 26 to Federal Highway 20 to State Highway 120)	What interstate highway passes by Douglas? (25)	What river does interstate highway 80 cross over? (Green River)	Which state borders Wyoming to the north? (Montana)
Which states border Wyoming to the east? (South Dakota and Nebraska)	Which states border Wyoming to the south? (Colorado and Utah)	Which states border Wyoming on the west? (Idaho, Montana, and Utah)	What federal highway would you take from Rawlins to get to Yellowstone National Park? (287)
What route would you take to get from Sheridan to Cody? (Interstate 90 to Federal Highway 14)	How far is Casper from Cheyenne? (177 miles)	How far is Rock Springs from Laramie? (208 miles)	How far is Riverton from Casper? (120 miles)
How far is Riverton from Yellowstone National Park? (183 miles)	What is the capital of Wyoming? (Cheyenne)	What interstate highway enters Wyoming from South Dakota? (90)	What interstate highway enters Wyoming from Nebraska? (80)

Great Map Games Scholastic Professional Books